The Early Modern Englishwoman:
A Facsimile Library of Essential Works

Series I

Printed Writings, 1500–1640: Part 2

Volume 3

Eleanor Davies

The Early Modern Englishwoman: A Facsimile Library of Essential Works

Series I

Printed Writings, 1500–1640: Part 2

Volume 3

Eleanor Davies

Selected and Introduced by
Teresa Feroli

General Editors
Betty S. Travitsky and Patrick Cullen

Ashgate

Aldershot • Burlington USA • Singapore • Sydney

Published by
Ashgate Publishing Ltd
Gower House
Croft Road
Aldershot
Hants GU11 3HR
England

Ashgate Publishing Company
131 Main Street
Burlington
Vermont 05401
USA

Ashgate website: http://www.ashgate.com

British Library Cataloguing-in-Publication Data
Davies, Eleanor
The early modern Englishwoman : a facsimile library of essential works.
Part 2: Printed writings, 1500–1640: Vol. 3
1. English literature – Early modern, 1500–1700 2. English literature – Women authors 3. Women – England – History – Renaissance, 1450–1600 – Sources 4. Women – England – History – Modern period, 1600– – Sources 5. Women – Literary collections
I. Title II. Travitsky, Betty S. III. Cullen, Patrick Colborn, 1940– IV. Feroli, Teresa V. Warning to the dragon VI. All the kings of the earth shall prayse thee VII. Woe to the house
820.8'09287

Library of Congress Cataloging-in-Publication Data
The early modern Englishwoman: a facsimile library of essential works. Part 2. Printed writings, 1500–1640 / general editors, Betty S. Travitsky and Patrick Cullen.

See page vi for complete CIP Block 99–55935

The woodcut reproduced on the title page and on the case is from the title page of Margaret Roper's trans. of [Desiderius Erasmus] *A Devout Treatise upon the Pater Noster* (circa 1524).

ISBN 1 84014 216 2

Printed in Great Britain by Antony Rowe Ltd, Chippenham, Wiltshire

CONTENTS

Library of Congress Cataloging-in-Publication Data
Eleanor, Lady, d. 1652.
[Selections. 2000]
Eleanor Davies / selected and introduced by Teresa Feroli.
p. cm. – (The early modern Englishwoman. Printed writings, 1500–1640, Part 2 ; v. 3)
Contents: Warning to the dragon – All the kings of the earth shall prayse thee – Woe to the house.
ISBN 1–84014–216–2
1. Prophecies. I. Feroli, Teresa. II. Eleanor, Lady, d. 1652. Warning to the dragon. III. Eleanor, Lady, d. 1652. All the kings of the earth shall prayse thee. IV. Eleanor, Lady, d. 1652. Woe to the house. V. Title. VI. Series.

BR1725.E43 A25 2000
248.2'9–dc21

99–55935

PREFACE
BY THE GENERAL EDITORS

Until very recently, scholars of the early modern period have assumed that there were no Judith Shakespeares in early modern England. Much of the energy of the current generation of scholars has been devoted to constructing a history of early modern England that takes into account what women actually wrote, what women actually read, and what women actually did. In so doing the masculinist representation of early modern women, both in their own time and ours, is deconstructed. The study of early modern women has thus become one of the most important—indeed perhaps the most important—means for the rewriting of early modern history.

The Early Modern Englishwoman: A Facsimile Library of Essential Works is one of the developments of this energetic reappraisal of the period. As the names on our advisory board and our list of editors testify, it has been the beneficiary of scholarship in the field, and we hope it will also be an essential part of that scholarship's continuing momentum.

The Early Modern Englishwoman is designed to make available a comprehensive and focused collection of writings in English from 1500 to 1750, both by women and for and about them. The first series, *Printed Writings, 1500–1640*, provides a comprehensive if not entirely complete collection of the separately published writings by women. In reprinting these writings we intend to remedy one of the major obstacles to the advancement of feminist criticism of the early modern period, namely the unavailability of the very texts upon which the field is based. The volumes in the facsimile library reproduce carefully chosen copies of these texts, incorporating significant variants (usually in appendices). Each text is preceded by a short introduction providing an overview of the life and work of a writer along with a survey of important scholarship. These works, we strongly believe, deserve a large readership—of historians, literary critics, feminist critics, and non-specialist readers.

The Early Modern Englishwoman will also include separate facsimile series of *Essential Works for the Study of Early Modern Women* and of *Manuscript Writings*. It is complemented by *Women and Gender in Early Modern England, 1500–1750*, a series of original monographs on early modern gender studies, also under our general editorship.

New York City
2000

INTRODUCTORY NOTE

Lady Eleanor Davies was born in 1590 to George Touchet, Baron Audeley, and his wife, Lucy. Although Lady Eleanor's was not one of the premier aristocratic families in England, she frequently invoked her noble patronymic as a source of her authority:

> ELEANOR DAVIES, handmayden of the most high GOD of Heaven, this Booke brought forth by Her, fifth Daughter of GEORGE, Lord of CASTLEHAVEN, Lord AUDELEY, and Tuitchet. NO inferior PEERE of this Land, in Ireland the fifth EARLE.

Little is known about the conditions of Lady Eleanor's upbringing and education. Her biographer, Esther S. Cope, appeals to the content of Lady Eleanor's treatises to speculate that she may have had training in Latin in addition to exposure to classical and modern authors. What is known is that, despite her noble rank, Lady Eleanor's life was mired in both flamboyant personal conflict and in the notoriety of the Castlehaven scandal, and that her writings were embroiled in political affairs.

In 1609, Lady Eleanor married the poet and prominent barrister Sir John Davies, to whom she bore three children. Of her children, only her daughter, Lucy, survived into adulthood. Lucy proved to be a great support to her mother and, on several occasions, petitioned for Lady Eleanor's release from jail. Sir John, preoccupied with his own career ambitions, discouraged his wife in the early stages of her prophetic career and burned one of her first treatises. She responded by telling Sir John 'within three years to expect the mortal blow', and he died shortly thereafter in 1626. When her second husband, the soldier Sir Archibald Douglas, burned her prophetic writings, she cryptically predicted that '*worse then death should befal*' him. By her account, this prediction was fulfilled when, during church services, Sir Archibald was 'strooken bereft of his sences, in stead of speech made a noice like a Brute creature'.

While the initial stages of Lady Eleanor's prophetic career were informally censured, her second publishing effort landed her in jail. In 1633, she travelled to Amsterdam to find a printer willing to produce her treatises. Once she returned to England and began to distribute her newly printed tracts, Archbishop Laud ordered them burned. Beyond destroying her books, Laud oversaw her trial before the Commission for Causes Ecclesiastical at which the judges determined that her writings 'much unbeseemed her Sex'. Her two years in prison did not deter her, and she was jailed again in 1637 for banding together with a group of women to protest the 'Romish' rituals practised at the Cathedral of Lichfield. The spectacular nature of her defiance – she occupied the bishop's throne, declared herself 'primate and metropolitan', and defaced the Cathedral's tapestries – only served to re-enforce earlier accusations of her madness and resulted in her being committed to Bedlam.

The prophetic career of Lady Eleanor spans the years between 1625 and 1652. During that time, she published some sixty-nine treatises, spent years in jail, and made astonishing predictions on subjects ranging from the coming of the apocalypse to the death of her first husband. Viewed as both an inspired seer and a mad 'ladie' by her contemporaries, Lady Eleanor has recently received a great deal of scholarly attention, not least of all because of her densely allusive and complex prose style.

In terms of her literary output, Lady Eleanor's most productive years came between 1641 and 1652 when she published sixty-six of her sixty-nine treatises. (These texts will appear in the next series of this facsimile library, *Printed Writings, 1641–1700*.) Although the easing of censorship restrictions in this period clearly enabled her to publish with greater freedom, she continued to encounter official rebuke and found herself in and out of jail in the years between 1646 and 1651. Lady Eleanor died on 5 July 1652. Lucy commemorated her mother's life with an epitaph that appropriately testified to Lady Eleanor's unswerving commitment to her prophetic vocation:

In a woman's body a man's spirit, In most adverse circumstances a serene mind, In a wicked age unshaken piety and uprightness. Not for her did Luxury relax her strong soul, or Poverty narrow it: but each lot with equal countenance And mind, she not only took but ruled.

A Warning to the Dragon and all his angels (1625)

In many ways, Lady Eleanor's first published prophetic treatise, *Warning*, is a classic example of the kind of apocalyptic writing that predominated in late sixteenth- and early seventeenth-century England. An anti-Catholic polemic which claims that the final vision of Daniel predicts the 'day of Judgement', *Warning* embraces the zeal for calculating the end of time and the militant Protestant rhetoric characteristic of the genre.

Within the context of Lady Eleanor's canon, *Warning* functions as something of a Rosetta stone. Because it does not possess the complex syntax of many of her later treatises, it is one of the most accessible of her writings, and it introduces the emphasis on signature and the preoccupation with England's past and present monarchs that figure prominently in her later work.

Lady Eleanor opens *Warning* by representing her signature anagram – 'Eleanor Audeley, Reveale O Daniel' – as an attempt to 'maske' her name. Of the numerous anagrams she employed throughout her career, 'Reveale O Daniel' appears most frequently and typically functions not to 'maske' her name in any way but to assert that her family name (as opposed, tellingly, to either of her married names) possesses hidden properties which link her to the prophet Daniel.

A second signature event of *Warning* comes when Lady Eleanor professes to have determined the meaning of the final vision of Daniel which enables her to predict that 'the day of Judgement' will take place 'nineteene yeares and a halfe' from 28 July 1625. (Her later texts identify the execution of William Laud, Archbishop of Canterbury, in January of 1645 as ringing in the 'day of Judgement' anticipated by *Warning*.) This prediction appeared in thirteen of her texts and came to be portrayed in her later treatises as the product of a 'Heavenly voice'. Thus, over time, what was once an act of divinely inspired calculation emerged as the moment of recognition when she received a literal call to prophesy.

Another leitmotif of Lady Eleanor's canon that first appeared in *Warning* is her celebration of the recently deceased prophet-king James I (himself the author of an anti-Catholic, exegetical treatise on Revelation) as a warrior who had struggled to suppress the reign of the Pope. She published *Warning* in the year James died and his son, the ill-fated Charles I, assumed the throne. In the hope that he would continue his father's work, Lady Eleanor dedicated *Warning* to Charles. The events of the late 1620s and early 1630s, however, left her disenchanted with Charles whom she later represented as Rome's champion rather than its foe.

The fine copy of *Warning* reproduced here comes from the British Library. Additional copies can be found at the Bodleian; Chatsworth, Bakewell, Derbyshire; and Trinity College, Dublin.

All the kings of the earth shall prayse thee (1633)

All the kings is one of three texts that Lady Eleanor had printed in Amsterdam in 1633, and, like *Warning*, *All the kings* is an exegetical treatise on the visions of Daniel. Visually, *All the kings*, with its reproduction of the Biblical text and its marginal commentary on specific passages, is reminiscent of the Geneva Bible and its important marginal commentaries.

One of the most interesting features of *All the kings* is its dedicatory letter to Elizabeth, Queen of Bohemia. Elizabeth was the daughter of James and the sister of Charles, and Lady Eleanor apparently turned to her, rather than to Charles, as the true heir to the dead king's theological legacy. This dedication probably stemmed from the deterioration of Lady Eleanor's esteem for Charles in 1628 after she had accurately predicted the month of the assassination of his most trusted advisor, George Villiers, Duke of Buckingham. Shortly thereafter, she had moved to St James in order to be near the Court for the purpose of 'pressing Great *Britains* blow'. Her move antagonized Charles, and he sent one of his servants to determine what she had 'to do with his affairs' and to warn her that if she 'desisted not, he would take another course'. In *All the kings*, Lady Eleanor signalled her disregard for Charles by appearing to suggest that she had written *Warning* for James but that, due to his death, she was unable to present it to him: 'intended to the King of chiefe memory your father … obtained not access, for with his fathers, the holy King was fallen asleepe.' Beyond disowning Charles as the 'true' dedicatee of her inaugural prophetic tract, she suggests that the recent death of Elizabeth's husband, Frederick, the Elector Palatine (in November of 1632) has made the Queen a likely patron of prophets. Lady Eleanor created the anagram 'ZAREP:VILAG' from one of the Elector Palatine's titles, the Palsgrave (or, as she spells it, 'Palizgrave'): 'ZAREP:VILAG' invokes the Phoenician town (village/VILAG?) of Zarephath to which God directed Elijah (I Kings 17) with the promise that he would receive hospitality at the hands of a widow. In light of the restrictions Lady Eleanor's husbands attempted to impose upon her prophetic career, it is not entirely surprising that she defined Elizabeth's new role as guardian of the Word in terms of her widowed status. (As yet another example of Lady Eleanor's career-long disdain for husbands, it strengthens the case for referring to her as Lady Eleanor, rather than by the surname of either of her husbands.)

The text of *All the kings* reproduced here is the only extant copy, and it comes from London's Public Record Office.

Woe to the House (1633)

Woe to the House is the first of Lady Eleanor's four treatises that defended the innocence of her brother, Mervin Touchet, Baron Audeley, Earl of Castlehaven, who was tried and executed in 1631 for raping his wife and sodomizing his servants. A broadside, *Woe to the House* bears the image of the Stanley coat of arms enclosed between two anagrams that vilify two Stanley women, Elizabeth and Anne. Through the anagram 'A LYE SATAN' and her transcription of I Kings 21, Lady Eleanor suggests that Castlehaven's second wife, Anne Stanley, is a type of Jezebel because she testified against Castlehaven and thus condemned, through her 'lies', an innocent Naboth. According to Cope, the Elizabeth of 'THAT JEZEBEL SLAIN' was Elizabeth Stanley, Countess of Huntingdon, the sister of Anne Stanley and mother-in-law of Lady Eleanor's now married daughter, Lucy Hastings. Since Sir John's death in 1626, Lady Eleanor had been engaged in a series of legal battles with her daughter's in-laws over their claims to her late husband's property. From Lady Eleanor's perspective, the Countess of Huntingdon had also, like her sister Anne, played the role of Jezebel. Lady Eleanor accuses the Countess of prompting 'two men' (Sir George Hastings and Thomas Gardiner) 'to beare witnesse against' her.

The fine text of *Woe to the House* reproduced here comes from London's Public Record Office. Another copy can be found at Worcester College, Oxford.

(Although a third text by Lady Eleanor, *Given to the Elector*, was first printed in 1633, a facsimile is not included in this volume because no extant copies survive from its original 1633 printing. *Given to the Elector* does exist, however, in reprint versions of 1648 and 1651, and will be included among the works by Lady Eleanor reproduced in *Printed Writings, 1641–1700*.)

References

STC 903.5 [*All the kings*], 904 [*Warning*], 904.5 [*Woe to the House*]

Berg, Christine and Philippa Berry (1981), '"Spiritual Whoredom": An Essay on Female Prophets in the Seventeenth Century' in *1642: Literature and Power in the Seventeenth Century: Proceedings of the Essex Conference on the Sociology of Literature, July 1980*, Francis Barker et al. (eds), Colchester: University of Essex

Cope, Esther S. (1992), *Handmaid of the Holy Spirit*, Ann Arbor: University of Michigan Press

Cope, Esther S. (ed.) (1995), *Prophetic Writings of Lady Eleanor Davies*, New York: Oxford University Press

Feroli, Teresa (1994), 'The Sexual Politics of Mourning in the Prophecies of Eleanor Davies', *Criticism* 36

— (1994), 'Sodomy and Female Authority: The Castlehaven Scandal and Eleanor Davies's *The Restitution of Prophecy* (1651)', *Women's Studies* 24

Hindle, C. J. (1936), 'A Bibliography of the Printed Pamphlets and Broadsides of Lady Eleanor Douglas the Seventeenth-Century Prophetess', *Edinburgh Bibliographical Society Transactions* 1:1

Mack, Phyllis (1992), *Visionary Women: Ecstatic Prophecy in Seventeenth-Century England*, Berkeley: University of California Press

Matchinske, Megan (1993), 'Holy Hatred: Formations of the Gendered Subject in English Apocalyptic Writing, 1625–51', *English Literary History* 60

Nelson, Beth (1985), 'Lady Elinor Davies: The Prophet as Publisher', *Women's Studies International Forum* 8

Purkiss, Diane (1992), 'Producing the voice, consuming the body: Women prophets of the seventeenth century' in *Women, Writing, History 1640–1740*, Isobel Grundy and Susan Wiseman (eds), Athens, Georgia: The University of Georgia Press

Spencer, Theodore (1938), 'The History of an Unfortunate Lady', *Harvard Studies and Notes in Philosophy and Literature* 20

Wiseman, Sue (1992), 'Unsilent Instruments and the Devil's Cushions: Authority in Seventeenth-Century Women's Prophetic Discourse' in *New Feminist Discourses*, Isobel Armstrong (ed.), London: Routledge

Wright, S. G. (1932–34), 'Dougle Fooleries', *Bodleian Quarterly Record* 7.75

TERESA FEROLI

Warning to the Dragon (*STC* 904) is reproduced from The British Library copy, Shelfmark 1016.e.22. The text-block of the original is 142 mm from 'a' of 'mans' in 1st line to final line (sig. C1r).

14.

A VVARNING TO THE DRAGON AND ALL HIS ANGELS.

***

LVKE, XXI.

Take heed to your selues, lest at any time your hearts be over-charged with Surfetting and Drunkennesse, and the Cares of this life, and so that day come upon you vnawares. For as a SNARE *shall it come on all them, that dwell on the face of the whole Earth.*

Marke yee this wicked persons, & yee friends of the vnrighteous MAMMON.

A SNARE O DEUIL.

Printed. M.DC.XXV.

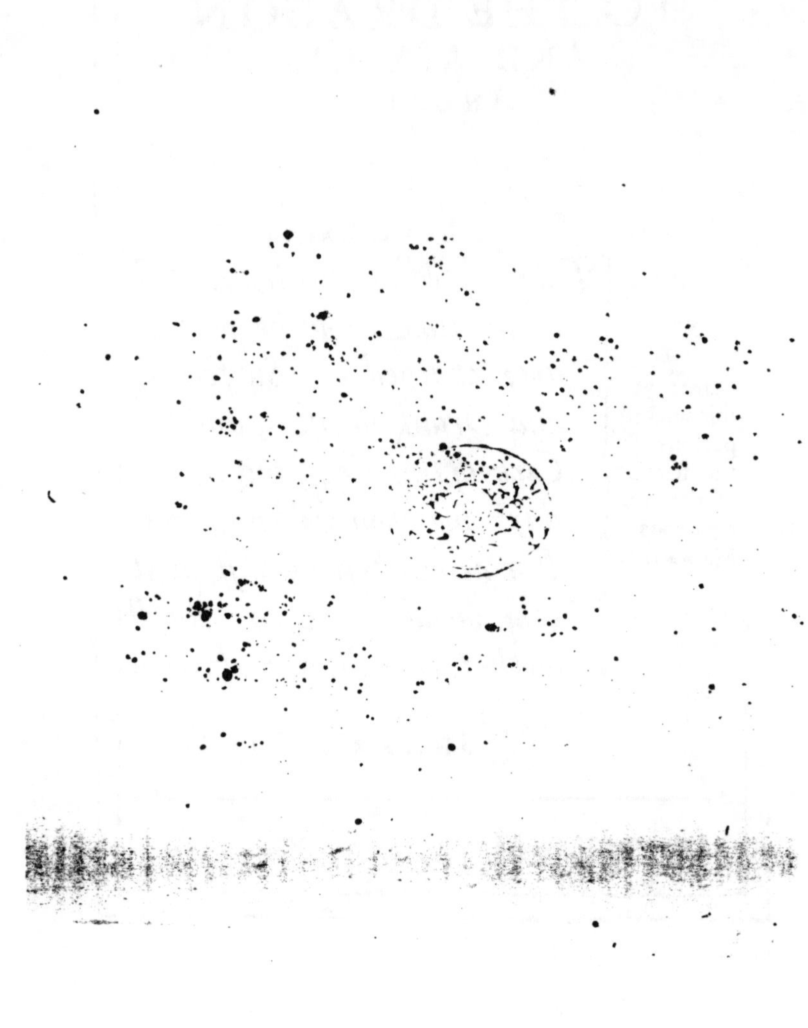

A Generall Epistle,

TO

The fold and Flocke of Christ,

and to them that are gone astray, that say they are Apostles and Catholiques and are not, &c.

Race be to you and Peace from God the Father, and from our Lord Iesus Christ, *who gaue himselfe for our Sinnes; and in the absence of his Body for a remembrance the Blessed Supper, till his second appearing. As often as we taste thereof, he takes it as a token we are not vnmindfull of his tender mercy that tasted Death it selfe for vs; so many melting trials and torments, the innocent Lambe for a brood of Vipers, whose damme is Death*

whose sting is Sinne, he that washed vs in his owne Blood vnto whome there is no accesse but by Faith; Behold hee commeth, and euery eye shall see him. To him be glory and dominion for euer and euer. Amen.

It seemed good vnto me, hauing a perfect vnderstanding giuen mee in these things, and the dispensation of them; an office not a trade; to roote out, to pull downe, to build, and to plant, by the grace and bounty of IESUS *our Lord God. To present this Visitation to your view, ioyning you together of the first Arke, and vniuersall great House, vessels of Honor and dishonor, some cleane and purified; others hauing need of purging.*

Former things are come to passe, and new things I declare vnto you; no age so weake, nor sex excusing; when the

Lord ſhall ſend and will put his words in their Mouth. He powreth out his Spirit vpon his hand-maidens; the rich are ſent emptie away, euen ſo Father for it ſeemed good in thy ſight.

Preſſed and conſtrained with obedience to him, and Duty towards you; ſaying no other things then the Prophets and Apoſtles did ſay ſhould come to paſſe, that yee might know the certainty of thoſe things, wherein yee haue beene inſtructed, whether you will heare or whether you will forbeare.

It is a ſalue to annoint and open the eyes of the blinde, to bring them that ſit in darkeneſſe a light, to leade them out of the Priſon-houſe; others by meanes of remembrance, (whoſe annoynting long ſince teacheth them all thinges) to ſtirre them vppe;

It is a true looking-glasse, a large houre-glasse, Phisicke for the sicke, wholsome for the whole, milke for the young, and meate for the strong. It is vpon Record due, an olde debt One and Twenty hun- yeares since; Vnto me is giuen this stone to polish, vnto me this grace is giuen.

It is as it were a new Song to be sung before the euerlasting Throne, a salutation for Strangers and the Brethren; if we loue them that loue vs, if we salute the Brethren only, what doe wee more then others; yea but they come at the last houre, others hauing borne the heate and burthen of the Day.

Shall not the lost Son be found againe, the Father of these that Blaspheme and are found lyers; But in the eye of our weakenesse their prosperitie will weaue the webbe of enuie; murmure not at the

the

good-man of the House; Is it not lawfull; is it not wrong (as he will) to dispose the riches of his owne goodnesse; nay, rather may we not all say, we are vnprofitable, we haue both gon out of the way, there is none that doth good, no not one; nay, are not his Iudgements according to truth; O man grudge not his grace, dispute not his justice.

But they haue bin, and will be to the worlds end, our persecutors and slaunderers, need they not so much the more our Prayers; recompence no-man euill for euill; Therefore let the Congregations of the faithfull Pray for them, poore, blind, distracted, naked, wretched people, and giue glory to God, who hath done away the vaile from these hidden mysteries, that hindred our stedfast sight, Though to blinde mindes and deafe harts, this vaile remaines still vntaken away.

Wherein for mine owne part, I challenge little, not so much as those that brought to the Tabernacle guifts of their owne spinning of Blew and other colours; But rather to be in the number of those servants, that drew out the wonderfull Wine for the Bridegroomes Feast, to beare it to the Gouernor and the Guests; though to cast in my myte with others I was never unwilling.

Finally, to those that require a Signe, or thinke this Confidence; Boasting that high stiles are not steps for the declining age of this weake world to climbe, my defence is no shorter then free.

Least any should thinke of me aboue or better then he seeth me to be, as others to suspect a forged passe; To present you with Pearles of that sort or holy things, I forbeare at this time.

If the debt be paid the secret of the multiplyed oyle is to my selfe; Though I shut the Doore or shadow my name, I feare no faces, smiles nor frownes, for. the hope of Israel, *to me no chaines are heavie, it is no bought nor stolne fire, my ability nor boldnesse extending so high; yet a Candle too high mounted for Sathan, and all his attempts to blowe it out, thrived the Gospell the lesse, rejected of the* Iewes.

But all alike hit not the marke, they presse forward; wranglers started aside like a broken Bowe, the match is wonne, one Foord is not knowne to all Passengers; eleven strikes the clocke saith he, twelve saith she; doe these contradict those that are not against vs or with vs; Antichristians those that are not against vs, are with vs; Even so, glory be to him alone (the Set is ours) the houre and set time of whose Iudgement is at hand; and O Lord remember thy servants Abraham, Isaac, *&* Iacob, *& looke not to the stubbornnes, nor to the wickednes of this People, turne their harts, preserue thy Church, and his victorious Ma*[tie]. *to tread downe the power of his enemies, our Soveraigne gratious Lord and the Queene, anoint them with thy holy Spirit, Crowne them with Grace; and forren Princes, especially the Kings excellent Sister, with a happie life here, and eternall life hereafter. Be gratious to the remnant of* IOSEPH, *heare I beseech thee the Prayer of thy servant.*

The Servant of Iesus Christ:

O A SVRE DANIEL.

DANIEL, — I END AL.

Postscript *TO maske my name with boldnesse to vnmaske Error I craue no Pardon, the manner let none dispise; Dreames in times past haue beene interpreted, our Fathers in divers manners haue beene spoken vnto, the winde bloweth where it listeth.*

ELEANOR AVDELEY

REVEALE O DANIEL,

TO

THE GREAT PRINCE, the King of *Great* BRITAINE, FRANCE, and IRELAND, Defender of the Faith.

THE INTERPRETATION OF THE VISIONS OF THE PROPHET DANIEL, *revealing the Man of Sinne; And the Morning Starre, before the comming of the Day.*

N the Visions of this Prophet are revealed the same things contained in the Revelatiō, which GOD gaue to Iesus Christ, to shew vnto his Servants things which must shortly come to passe; things that are not, to bring to nought things that are: And as he signified to his beloved Servant IOHN, the Contents of the secret Booke by his Angell; Even so the Lambe slaine by the eternall Decree purposed from the foundation of the world; Declared the same things to the man greatly beloved, his servant DANIEL, vnfolded in this present exposition; drawing the juice of many sorts wanting roome and leasure, to lay things in order, wherein the Scripture will repaire the want of methode. Being not willing for the lighting of a Match to make a fire, when the stroke of a Flint is of more facilitie; Speaking not to a People of a strange Speech and of a hard Language, but to the House of *Israell*; Avoyding mans enticing words; things without life, giue no life, that revealeth not the testimony of IESUS; at whose Name, a name aboue every name, Let every knee bowe. Heare all yee Children of my people, harken O Earth!

The first vision of this holy Prophet, was in the I. yeare of the raigne of BELSHAZZER, King of Babilon; from which spirituall Babilon takes the denomination. One and Twentie hundred yeares since.

Wherein he ſaw the foure Windes of Heaven, or the loſed Angels bound in the great River *Euphrates* the auntient bounds of the great Roman Empire, that ſtroue vpon the great Sea, and the foure great Beaſts, that came vp from the Sea diuers one from another. Theſe blowing Windes had no power to hurt, till the ſervants of God were Sealed in the foreheads, at what time that Cõmonwealth became a Monarchy, perſecuting the Church of God being then with Child, Trauailing in birth, crying and pained to be deliuered of the man Childe, roaring like a Lyon, the whole Forreſt ringing, ruling all Nations with a Rod of Iron; that breaketh in pieces and ſubdueth all things: He is *Alpha* and *Omega*, ſo haue the ſervants of God a Two-fold ſence. Beſides man including ſome other of his Creatures, bearing the names of men, yet being neither Man nor Beaſt; Praiſe yee him Sun and Moone, &c.

I heard the number of them: And here ended the Sealing of the firſt Covenant, a yoake which our Fathers were not able to beare, to eſtabliſh the ſecond, which is Spirituall, to put his Lawes in their mindes, with the Pensell of his Grace to write them in their hard harts, a light Burthen, for the letter of the Law, graven in stone is the sentence of death; But the Spirit giveth life to stony harts, that were dead in trespasses and sinnes; yea, the whole valley of dead Bodies, turn'd into Stones and Earth, from Abell the first Borne, to the last man taken vp in the Field, they are all holy vnto the Lord, their iniquitie is forgiven and forgotten, as a Father, hee remembreth their sinne no more.

Of these were Sealed to bee of the seed of Abraham, one hundred forty and foure Thousand, twelue times twelue Thousand: Of which faithfull Number Iesvs Christ the Saviour of the world, the only begotten Sonne of the living GOD, in the likenesse of sinfull Flesh without Sinne, the Lyon of the Tribe of *Iudah*, was sealed on the Eight day of his Nativitie; The Lyonesse bringing but one, and but once in her life.

That with the sprinckling and shedding of his Blood, both Covenants might be sealed: These were the first Fruits vnto God, and to the Lambe, hauing the Token of the everlasting Covenant, of the great mysterie in those times, concerning CHRIST and his Church, put in the Flesh a Figure of the Heart.

Which first Covenant remaines to vs a Patterne of tendernes, not made with hands, the Heart by a mutuall respect being now the Closet or secret part, whereby wee Gentiles are made the tender Spouse, the habitation of God, fellow heires of the vnsearchable Riches, joyned to Christ the head, that in times past were the Children of disobedience and wrath, Aliens from the common-wealth of *Israell*, Strangers from the Covenants of promise, having no hope (without God) in the world, are now, who were somtimes farre off; of all Nations, Kindreds and Tongues; vncircumcised Philistines, not of his Brethren; not of the House of his Father, By the blood of IESUS CHRIST made nigh members, of his Body, of his Flesh, and of his Bones; greater loue and felicitie can none expresse.

Of which great mysterie, Hipocrites, next

Harlots, whose counterfeit beautie deceiues not him, whose praise is of men, and not of God; false Gods, are no partakers; the outward Token, being common to both. To assure vs of which, receiving the earnest of his Spirit, that abideth, not crying Master; Carest thou not, that wee perish; but Abba, Father.

Thus our tackling lost, without Anchor, to repayre the ruines and weaknesse of these decayed, stinke weather-tempest driven bottomes, such Treasures of Millions expended and bestowed, what burthen, what prizes, what things God hath prepared to bee the lading of these vessels of honour; Eye hath not seene, eare hath not heard, neither hath entred into the hart of man: To which, all the Transported affections felt or fained, injoyed without paines or feare, may seeme but light dotage, as Light and Darknesse compared, compared with the Crowne and weight of that Eternall blisse.

The Foure windes prepared for an houre, and a day, and a moneth, and a yeare; are the powers of these foure great Beasts; shewing their degrees of residence; also the finall Blast is included ; The Sea are the Nations of the Earth.

The beginning and the ending, thus saith hee to the Sea : Waues drowning one another, swelling into Mountaines, for glory foaming out your owne shame. Saying, haile to the Wood awake, according to your owne vnderstanding, you haue made Idols and Images, not by my direction, but after the invention of the Craftsman, and haue exalted your hearts and forgotten mee, giving my Praise to graven Images, and my glory to another for your God, (not setting me before your eyes) you haue gotten a Divell, a false Prophet, whom I sent to proue you ; that takes my lawes in his mouth, not of loue, but for strife and envie : Thinkes he to say ; Lord, Lord, in thy Name wee haue cast out Divels, Preached, and Baptized ; my answer is not vnknowne to you both, though you thinke to plead ignorance, persecuting and dispising the number of my little ones.

You onely haue I knowne, of all the Families of the Earth, whose transgressions doe hasten your Iudgement; Therefore I will punish you for your iniquities, you shall bee like the Morning Cloud, and the early dew that passeth away as the Chaffe that is driven with a scattering whirle-winde out of the Flower, as smoake out of a Chimney vanishing away; And I will bee like a Lyon, as a Leopard by the way I will wayte and obserue you, and as a Beare that is bereaued of her Whelpes, I will teare the Kall from your harts and devoure you, But to the faithfull I will bee a King, a Saviour; as an Eagle stirring vp her Nest, fluttering over her young, bearing them vpon the wing; So I will preserue mine inheritance, my Portion as the Apple of mine eye.

These are the words of the First, that was like a Lyon, his strength shall overcome the rest, and take their Dominion away, having no number or finite parts expressed; the time of whose vndeuided Kingdome is infinite and alwaies; As his yeares haue no end, his Crownes are many; This is the Lyon of the Tribe of *Iudah*, having of Flesh a tender hart; a mans hart was giuen vnto it; The Prince of the Kings of the Earth, the first and the last; And because he is the roote, and made of the seed of DAVID; Hee is here accompted amongst these Beasts; This is hee that sate vpon the white Horse, the Circle of the Earth, to iudge and make War; beholding the Inhabitants like Grasshoppers; and a Bowe and a Crowne was giuen vnto him; Hee is the Lord of Lords, the King of Kings, and of his Kingdome there is no end.

The second Beast like a Beare, the Seauenth head, that had Three ribbes in the Mouth betweene the Teeth of it, signifying, Three hundred yeares; this is the deuouring Raigne of the Heathen Romaine Emperours, which lasted so long, licked by the Diuell; In the Infancie of which Empire, the Sonne of God was Crucified, and the Citie of Ierusalem destroyed, wherein the yearely Sacrifice or feast of the Passouer was solemnized, that in her might be found the Blood of Prophets and Saints, and of all that were slaine vpon the Earth, in which first seuentie yeares, the Apostles and seuentie finished their testimony what they had seene and heard, after which followed the ouer-spreading of abomination spoken of by our Sauiour, making the Sanctuary desolate, defiled with Carkasses which can neither see, heare, nor walke, abominable carrion, the house of Prayer, made the Gallery of the Diuell, for his deuices to stand in.

And this is hee that sate vpon the Red Horse, Hauing a great Sword giuen vnto him, to make Warre with the Church of God, deuouring much Flesh, Burning, Scorching it with fire, Haile mingled with Blood, destroying Trees, and all greene grasse, smote euery Herbe, and brake euery Tree; and here ended the first Woe with this second Beast, all fire and horrible Cruelty, such as there was none like it in all the Land of spirituall Egypt since it became a Nation, and shortly after began the next Woe, where the fire is not mentioned, because the smoake is so great, thicke darkenesse or heresie, false doctrine extinguishing the Light of truth, which shall continue vntill the third Woe, Hell fire, and Brimstone or Blasphemy, issuing out of their Mouthes, a great crye from him that sits vpon the Throne, when Rednesse shall be turn'd into Palenesse to the Maide behinde the Mill, the Captaine in the Dongeon, free and bond, because of the last Plague the second Death.

The third Beast that was like a Leopard, or halfe a Lyon, an Ape betweene Man and beast, whose feete or first footing, were as the feete of a Beare, that had vpon the back of it foure Wings, like a Fowle or painted Bird: Two of the Eagle, and two of the Dragon; signifying his time, Foure hundred yeares before the comming in of Antichrist, then came the King of *Babylon* to Ierusalem, and besieged it, taking the advantage of the Night, what Linkes or Torches brought him thither I reade not, but Moonlight there was little, though hee were on his way or Wing, but letted Two hundred yeares before.

Bearing also foure heads, foure standing vp for it, shewing the deuision of the Empire into so many parts, being then too

large and great for the gouernment of one man. This is the Dragon of Egipt; that Monarchy that began with the Christian Emperours, whose deadly wound (Death to the Soule) was washed in the Blood, and healed by the Stripes of the heauenly Samaritan; There is now no healing of the Bruise, it is putrified, the Wound is grieuous; the Leopard cannot change his spots; binde thy Tyre vpon thy head, forbeare to cry: O Virgin daughter of Egipt, in vaine shalt thou goe vp into Gillead and take Balme, or vse Medicines, thou dost runne in vaine. And this is hee that sate vpon the blacke Horse; the Ethiopian cannot change his skinne, lesse man then the *Minataure*; more Monster then a *Centaure*, ingendred of black Cloudes; carried about of every Winde, to whom is reserued the Blacknesse of Darknesse for ever: Blacke will take no other hew; hauing a payre of Ballances given into his hand, without respect of persons, to measure to all men, rich and poore, free and bond, a measure of Wheate for a penny, and three measures of Barley for a penny; Hoe! every one that thirsteth, and hee that hath no money, Come buy and eate, giue not your money for stones in stead of Bread, say not Ignorance is better then Knowledge, Neither hurt the Oyle and the Wine; Touch not the Lords annointed, and doe his Prophets no harme, that Nourish you with truth and vnderstanding.

The last Beast the fourth, that is the Eight, and was Seven heads and is not, and is of the Seven, and goeth into perdition, that had great Iron Teeth, that devoured and brake in peeces, and stamped the residue with the feete thereof, and was divers from all the Beasts that were before it; having a Miter of Tenne hornes, signifying also, though the Crownes be not here expressed, so many hundred yeares his Limitted time, the Tenne dayes of tribulation in the Apocalips, wherein the Divell shall haue power to cast the faithfull into Prison; (After the Tribulation imediately of those dayes; Two shall be in the field, *&c.*) Nine of which number are expired, and some part of the last hundred, but how many are to come; by these hornes precisely cannot be aymed at without the Art or Science of Chronologie; This is *Iudas* the Divell, the King of *Babilon* and Egypt, the raigne of Antichrist Pope of *Rome*, count the Letters of his name for it is the nomber of his time, whose name is Death; hated mortally the King of *Rome* and *Italie*: This is hee that sate vpon the Pale Horse, the sonne of Perdition, of all Complexions the darkest, neerest to corruption, threatning alone, a hart charged with so much wickednesse and malice as the Red Horse, all the sanguines in the Rayne-bow, and the Sword cannot set out more of Bruitish crueltie; had he winges to his will, and of time length to the height and bignesse of his insatiable minde; NERO, TITVS, DOMITIANVS, these beasts of the Earth, their hearts and policies parraleld would seeme but a Curre coupled or compared with this greedy Woolfe. A Bull as bloudy as the Beare.

Whose land is covered with Locusts and Darknes; even darknes that may bee felt rising out of the depth of the bottomlesse pit of Sathans malice very grievous; yet had all the faithfull light in their dwellings that they might not loose the way; for it was Commanded these Armies of Scorpions besieging the holy City, hauing pernitious stings, both wayes voluptuous and malitious, The power of the Enemy that they should not hurt the grasse of the Earth, neither any greene thing, by any meanes nothing should hurt them, but only drye Trees or boughs, bearing no fruite of repentance, those men that haue not the Seale of God in their gracelesse foreheads, that they should not kill these wretched blinde miserable People, but that they should bee tormented fiue Moneths, as in those dayes the most part, most Lamentable in the siege of *Ierusalem* by Famine were tormented so long compassed with a Trench, kept in on every side, Seeking death, and desiring to dye, &c.

This did the Lord because the Princes of Egipt, harkened not to milde Moses, but hardened their harts, and did evill in the sight of the Lord, after the Abominations of the Heathen; Therefore saith the Lord,

I am against thee ô Dragon, which lyest in the Hart (the middest of the Rivers) which said my Riuers are mine owne, I haue made it for my selfe; I will put hookes in thy Clawes, and leaue the Throne into the Wildernesse, where there is no water; and all the Inhabitants shall know that I am the Lord, because they haue beene a staffe of Reede to the house of *Israel*, when they tooke hold of thee by the hand, thou didst breake and Rent all their shoulder; and when they leaned on thee, thou brakest, and made all their loynes to be at a stand, with the Burthens of Bricke and Rubbish thy Officers did lay vpon them.

Thou hast giuen them Stubble for Straw, vapor of smoake for Victuall; thou hast made their liues bitter vnto them; Therefore the Lord is against thee whose healed Wound is festred, turned wilde againe, become Antichristian and incureable, thou that haddest the Ballances in thine owne hand; **Thou that art like a Leopard or a young Lyon of the Nations, as a Dragon; or a Whale in the Seas, with thy Diadem** of Ten hornes, crowned with Ten Crowns, ſo many Antichriſtian hundred yeares, Nine of which accompt are caſt, paſt, and expired.

Troubling the waters with thy feete, and fowleſt their Rivers; the whole Sea of *Rome*, the third part of the maine Sea is become Blood; Behold the Lord is againſt thee and againſt thy Rivers, which are turned into Wormwood (woe due O *Rome*) and Hemlocke; Even the Third part of the waters, the ſtreames of Iuſtice and Mercy are become poyſon and Bitterneſſe; I hate and deſpiſe your Images, Feaſt dayes, Proceſſions, Solemne aſſemblies, ſaith the Lord; who required thoſe things: I cõmanded, Iudgement ſhould runne downe free as water, and Righteouſneſſe as a mighty ſtreame; Woe the Bloody Citie.

You are impudent and diſobedient Children, as the day of your Viſitation, ſo are your ſinnes hidden from you, when you ſhall ſay for ſhame to the Mountaines Cover vs, and to the Rocks and Hills fall vpon vs; you will know your tranſgreſſion, the long Wings of the morning, the Caues of Makadah ſhall not preſerue you, Lightening, Thundring Cannons, the whole Globe at a ſhot, ſhiuering your Bodyes, ſinking your Soules, and making your harts to hop: Eare never heard, neither hath entred into the hart of man ſuch horror, forſaken of all, but the Divell and his Angells, burned and buried aliue, of all the Creatures not a drop of water remaining, of Light not a ſparke, Rebells these terrors as Shot or Haileſtones from Heaven Pell-mell, ſhall driue you into a Bottomleſſe gulfe headlong; the great day of his wrath is come, ſaying to the fiery Lake; Hide vs from the face of him that ſits vpon the Throne.

When the faithfull ſcattered People ſhod with the everlaſting Ghoſpell of Peace, after all their labours and travaile in this Wilderneſſe, ſhall enter into the Land of Reſt: Here is the Body of the Beaſt deſtroyed; Pharoah and all his Multitude of vnbeleeving Lowzie orders; even all his Hoſt of furious Horſemen as Locuſts, eating every herbe, and all the fruite of the Trees the haile had left, drowned in Hell Fyre the bottomlesse red Sea, that may boast rather of their Blaines and Boyles, then Vermin, which their owne Magitians denie not to be the manifest finger of God; vaunting they winne by their Cosening game term'd Chastitie, the Ioyes of heaven, and Secret bosome Almes in breeding Lice: Such vncleane Ragges past mending, I did meane to cast away, but since you will not heare MOSES and the Prophets, I will bestowe some labour to ayre them for you, and your patch'd Coates waxen olde and bad to make bags for heavenly Treasure, well may they stoppe Bottles when your Reward is weeping and gnashing of Teeth; in those dayes, all the Water I finde the Saints will supply you with, to coole your blistered Tongues.

Masters though to simple People you seeme to make straite steps, it is no newes to say you incline too much on the left hand. Thinke yee the Crownes like Gold can deceiue vs; or hayre as the hayre of Women; The vayle of shamefastnesse, shewing ſobriety and ſubiection: Thinke yee thoſe long locks like ſeparited Nazarites, can cover your notted crownes from the Raizer, or hide your pined Bodyes pinch'd of Provender like neighing Horſes prepared to the Battaile, It is not vnknowne to vs, the golden Cup, and theſe gilden counterfeit Crownes like falſe Haire to cover Baldneſſe; Both came out of one Furnace: they are yet vnpaid for.

Though Esau ſhould lend you Teares, yet ſhall yee come and worſhip before the feet of them, you now diſpiſe and perſecute; There is no bleſſing reſerved, the Mourning day is at hand, the Armour you beare ſhines with the Brotherly affection you beare vs, wee feare not your furie; Go yee Curſed, heere is your farewell, receiue the Portion of Hipocrites, and eate the fruit of Lyes reioycing and truſting in your owne counterfeit Righteouſneſſe, painted flames, ſuch falſe Coine will not paſſe. Eternall life is free guift purchaſed by Grace; receiue the wages of Sinne; venemous Armies, the power of the Enemie led by the Starre called *Worme-*

woald, To those that haue not drunke or smoak'd out their eyes, as visible as Lightning or a Lampe fallen from Heaven, threatning Warre, Famine, with Pestilent Mortalitie ; the fourth part, the whole Christian world infected by that strumpet Hagge *Rome* and *Italie*. Lastly, the name of his Palenesse was Death, because hee is the last, and Hell followed with them with deadly malice, Raigning till the day of Iudgement, after which hee shall swimme with his fellowes, and bathe in the Lake that burnes with Fire and Brimstone.

These three Beasts signified by the great Citie devided into Three parts, so many severall persecutions of the Church vnder great *Babylon*, With a bold stroake, the last is not drawne in cullours least to the life; the fourth Beast (the false Prophet, their Popes falleth ;) the bitter Starre turning Iudgement into Gaule of Aspes falne from Heaven, Signifying the losing of his Keyes, (pride will haue a fall) for which hee was cast out of the presence of God : God and Mammon cannot be served together ; here hath hee the command of the bottomlesse Pit, smoaking with Heresie and ignorance; The Keys of the Kingdome of Hell, which trust so much hee boasteth of, given him by the Dragon the Divell, to deçeiue them that dwell vpon the Earth; saying in the sight and opinion of men; Let it be knowne this day, that I haue done all these things at thy word; that these are thy Keyes; I am thy Apostle; and if I be the man of God, let fire come downe from Heaven and consume all those, that obey not my orders, and Lawes; and at what time yee heare the sound of my Instruments; fall downe and worship the Image, that I NABVCHADNEZAR haue set vp, whose breath is in my hand, and whole are all my wayes to glorifie mee; and who so falleth not down, &c,

This *Baals* Prophet the last Beast, having devoured and broken in peeces the Roman Empire, exercising all the power of him whose Rome he vsurpeth; the Lord saying, I that forme the Light, and create Darknesse; I that make Peace, and create evill, I will strengthen the Armies of the King of

Babilon, and put my Sword into his hand. But I will breake PHAROAHS Arme, and and he shall groane before him, with the groaning of a deadly wounded man; Moreover, thus saith the Lord of Hosts that keepes backe no mans pay.

The King of *Babilon* caused his Army to serue a great seruice against CHILDRIC King of *Tirus*, euery head was made Bald of his Race, and euery shoulder peel'd, yet had hee no wages for his Armie; Therefore the Land of Egypt shall bee his for his labour, because they wrought for mee saith the Lord; for there shall be no more a Prince in Egypt whose brightnesse was Excellent, and the forme thereof terrible to all the world, But rather a painted Image, a Vassoll, that the working of the poysoned Potion in the golden Cup, the mysterie of iniquitie bee not hindred, A base Kingdome the basest of all Kingdomes, neither shall it exalt it selfe any more aboue the Nations; for I will diminish them, it shall be no more the confidence of the house *Israell*.

Having now the spoyle of the Land for

his Armie and the Sword and Ballances in his owne hand to make a prey of mercy and truth, with his Hornes and heeles as weapons to warre and weare out the Saints given into his hand vntill a time and times; and the deviding of times, Three dayes and a halfe Two and fortie Moneths Three yeares and a halfe, halfe the mysticall weeke, vntill the Day of Iudgement; to make Merchandize of euery thing, that no man may buy or sell without his Marke, marked with his fiends foote; which is his Seale, the signet of the Fisherman that beareth the name of the Beast.

The nomber of his name is then the nomber of a man, which is the nomber of his Age or Dayes; but this is the nomber of his Moneths; Naturall Beasts not living so long, the yeares being not so many as the dayes are to few. As one saith, the nomber of his Moneths are with the Lord; Also halfe the mysticall Weeke is delivered by the same measure, The latter Six Moneths added to the former Six hundred, making as compleat Fiftie, as Threescore make Fiue yeares; Here is Wiſdome the counſell of times and ſeaſons revealed, according to the eternall purpoſe, which the wiſedome of the Father put in his owne power, God hath numbred thy Kingdome and finiſhed it, thou art weighed in the ballances, thou tyrant, that boaſteſt of thy wit, and art found wanting graines innumerable, thy Kingdome is divided, and given to the people of the Saints of the moſt Higheſt, whoſe Kingdome is an everlaſting kingdome &c. Therfore let him that readeth count this number well, and well marke, the marke of the Beaſt, is the Signet of the Fiſherman, which men take in their right hand, wherewith his Band are branded in the foreheads, and this is the Caractor and colours that diſtinguiſheth his Traine-Souldiers from the followers of the Truth.

Therefore thus ſaith the Lord to the King of *Babilon*, Antichriſt thy dayes be few, The great day of my wrath is at hand, even for the Elects ſake, and the Soules that reſt vnder the Altar, crying for Execution and Vengeance vpon thee, whoſe Bodyes thou haſt beheaded, burned and buryed aliue, slaine for the Testimony they held, the time is shortned, thy Bishoppricke shall bee voyde, and become a habitation for Divells; and because thou remembrest not to shew mercy, by swift destruction thy memorie shall be cut off from the Earth, thy Damnation slumbreth not, as a theefe in the night, and as a snare it shall come shortly vpon thee; Thou hast loved cursing, in blessing thou hast not delighted, but as a cloake for Covetousnesse, selling to thy Marchants for money, those foule oyntments to fill thy Bagge, calling and crying from thy Exchange and darke shoppe; if any man Thirst to commit Whoredom, spirituall or carnall, Treason, or Murther, let him come to mee and drinke of my Golden Cuppe, Incest or Parricide; *Hoc misterium firmiter profitemur*; what doe yee lacke; wee can sell you for Gold, Silver, and pretious stones, thin Wood, Brasse, Iron, and Marble, all manner of Vessells, in Nunneries or Stewes, what will yee giue; These execrable odors, and thy Brazen browed Bulls, casting flakes of Fire and fulminations in the ſight of men from their noyſome Noſtrills and Thundring throates, as with a Garment thou haſt cloathed thy ſelfe, thou haſt robbed mee even of this whole Nation, therefore prepare thy ſelfe thou curſed for everlaſting fire, prepared for the Divell and his Angells, which ſhall enter into thy Bowells like water, and ſoake with thine oyntments, as oyle into thy Bones, and mingle with thy marrow; thus let the Enemies of the Lord bee rewarded, yea, in the meane time let them be their own executioners.; let one IVDAS with Poyſon burſt out the Bowells of another; let their hope be as the giuing vp of the Ghoſt, and their righteouſneſſe wherein they truſt, in thy remembrance as water that paſſeth away; Let them curſe, but Bleſſe thou ô Lord to whom vengeance belongeth, ſhew thy ſelfe, lift vp thy ſelfe thou Iudge of the Earth, and to this proude man of Sinne render a reward.; let him not haue the vpper hand, ſitting vpon the Throne of Iniquitie in thy Temple, ſhewing himſelfe that hee is God, Conſume him ô Lord with the Breath of thy mouth, and destroy him quickly with the Brightnesse of thy comming.

Lastly, this Beast his habitation is compared to a woman for Sorceries, shamelesnesse and gorgious trimming, arrayed in Purple and Scarlet, the Virgin daughter of the King of *Egipt*, is become the Whore of the King of *Babilon*, the faithfull Citie is become a Harlot, hauing in her hand a Cuppe full of abominations, Witchcraft and Blasphemy, viz. worshipping Idols of Gold and and Silver, Brasse, Wood, and Stone, mixing holy things with filthy excrements, remission, the forgiuenesse of sinnes, and calling the foule Sinagogue of Sathan, the Church of God, and these are the spices and spirits wherewith her Cup is brewed; and this is the Golden Cuppe, wherewith the Kings of the Earth haue been made so drunken with, a Cup of *Sodome*, Wine mixed with the Blood of Dragons, and stirred with the stings of Aspes; Is this meate indeed, and drinke indeed, the sawce commeth after; Is this the true Mother; is this the Woman shee is taken for, with Eagles wings; her childe caught vp vnto God and to his Throne, and having a crowne of Twelue Starres; in no wise in her there is no Bowells of a Mother, though they striue to the end of the world.

Her Iudgement followeth; And a name was written vpon her forehead *BABILON*, The Mother of Harlots, and Abominations of the Earth, the Print is not small, yet not so large as the mysterie is deepe; It was written, and therefore to bee read: Thus, the hidden mystery of this Enigmaticall writing is here; the secret of numbers to teach vs to number her dayes; The numbers are these, and I heard the number of them, Two hundred thousand thousand horsemen, hauing breast-plates of fire and Gunpowder or hiacinth, force and furie in stead of faith and loue, alluding to the double number of NINVS Horsemen, wherewith he subdued so many Nations in Seventeene years: The double confirmation of this mysterie seventeene hundred yeares also, being the limited time fixed to finish her warre, which began with the Lambe, and ended in ſubduing his Saints and Servants; And as the fiery Army needing no fuell, were to the Army of NINVS, conſiſting of Twenty hundred Thouſand, amounting a hundred to one, ſo is the accompt of the time, when the ſpreading Vine of the Earth, the cluſters of her Grapes being ripe, ſhe ſhall be caſt into the great winepreſſe of the wrath of God. Theſe Tyrants, (here is wiſdome to looke into theſe accompts) ſhall make her deſolate and naked, and eate her fleſh, and burne her with fire, for God hath put it in their hearts to fulfill his will, when *Babylon* the glory of Kingdomes, ſhall be as *Sodome* and *Gomorah*, the time is neere, the dayes ſhall not bee prolonged.

The Father of this goodly Baby, (yet auncient, no novice in her whoredome) for ſo hee nameth himſelfe, there is no need to name him (at whoſe entrance the Fourth Angell or Winde was looſed) as hee is ſufficiently notorious, ſo is he miſtaken Sathan that old Serpent, begetting the Impe of Fornication, before ever the Beaſt and his falſe ſpouſe came together, deceivers as ſeldome wanting cloakes of craft to hide their ſhame, as their of-ſpring faile in Lyneaments and likeneſſe to their Parents, ſeven heads no leſſe markes then Mountaines, ſeeing as incredible as ſuperfluous and monſtrous, were it not the Evidence and demonſtration of that Sinagogue to proue her title and viſibilitie, drunken with the Blood of Saints and Martyrs, In ſteed of her Mothers milke and breaſt ſhee ſucks her hart-Blood, whoſe Father was a Lyer and a Murtherer from the beginning.

To Adminiſter the rites of their vnrighteous miſtery ; This City Bab , hath Citie Goſſips, NINEVY is not invited, ſhe repented at the Preaching of the poore Prophet, ſhee is none of them ; But *Babylon* for her Pride and impudency at this Antichriſtian ſolemnity or ſhew of Chriſtianitie ; The Mother of Harlots ; for her ſtiffe neck is preferred before her, whoſe name this ſhameleſſe place, never to be outworne or blotten out , beares in her fatall brazen forehead.

Besides, this Lady sitting vpon her Beast, seventeene Kings to beare vp her Traine, decked with Gold and pretious Stones, and Pearle, whose name is also *Semiramis* or *Iesabell*, for magnificence millions of men, viz. a hundred times Twenty hundred Thousand; Her Altars, Images, Sorceries, and Blood of Prophets and Saints, Saying in her hart, I sit a Queene and am no Widow; a Lady for ever, I am, and none else besides mee; there are Seven Kingdomes.

Fiue are fallen downe dead drunke, vpon whom the Lord hath poured out the spirit of deepe sleepe, and closed their eyes, they shall revert nor rise no more; After slumbering the other Two, (though they haue falne from the truth,) shall stagger and come to themselues againe; and that Must now growne sower and stale, their lust shall be little to taste thereof againe; The first Kingdome or ONE IS, are the Brittish Islands, the right Inheritance of King IAMES the first of that Name of Great *Britaine* and *Ireland*; for the Iles feared the Iudgement of the Lord and saw it; Even

the

the ends of the Earth were afraid and drew neere. The other is not yet come, and when it commeth, it can continue no long ſpace, the end of the world is ſo neere.

O ſenceleſſe poore Beaſts who hath bewitched you; why lye yee ſtill, who hath bitten you; ariſe, chooſe not Death rather then life; how are yee ſwolne, why ſhould your Carcaſſes be dung, and meate for the fowles of Heaven? Why will yee dye, ſtand vp; why goe yee backward; what aſtoniſhment is this that hath taken you; be recovered, vnderſtand, halt not, yet heare the word of the Lord; curſt cattell, backſliding Heifers hee delighteth in Mercy; provoke not him with your ſtrange vanities and Bruitiſh abominations; The day of the Lord is at hand.

Therefore awake yee Drunkards, weepe and howle all yee drinkers of Wine, becauſe of the new Wine the Deepe Cup, the day of the wrath of the Lord is at hand; yee Kings of the Earth and Rulers of *Sodome*, who haue commited fornication, and lived deliciouſly with this indulgent Witch, the mother of Harlots ; when yee see her brought to the stake and vtterly burnt with fire ; how will yee stand, for strong is the Lord who Iudgeth her ; what will yee say ; yee shall stand a farre off, or wish in vaine the Mountaines to cover you, howling and gnashing your Teethes for feare of her Torment, whose sinnes as the smoake of her Burning haue reached vp vnto Heaven ; saying alasse, alasse, *Sodome*, alasse, *Babylon*, *Rome* the great Citie, the head of the Monarchy ; for in the twinckling of an eye, an houre vnlookt for, thy Iudgement is come, is that a time to cast dust on your heads?

Never more shall we heare in thee the voyce of Harpers and Pipers, awaking and calling for rewards to Saints and our Lady; and Trumpeters when wee doe our Almes ; Never more shall wee see in thee Idolls or Images so auntient, the curious device of the Craftsman, nor the sound of the grinding Millstone ; our Altars decked as a shop, shining with the light of so many Tapers and Candles. Nor the voyce of the Bridegroome, called the head, and the Bride by

Prelates and so many Kings our holy Mother; The Net is spread, shee is taken in the Snare, in grinding the face of the Poore, shee that so much glorified her selfe, in a day and an houre her Plague is come.

The Thrones of these Earthly Kingdomes cast downe the auncient of dayes shall appeare; his long Traine, and the great white Throne whereon he sate, from whose Face the Earth and the Heavens vncleane in his sight fled away, in whose presence ministred Thousand thousands, and Ten thousand times Tenne Thousands; also the Two Witnesses are brought forth, the Books of the Law and the Prophets, to Iudge every man by his workes, or according to his faith, for if they beleeue not the writings of MOSES; how can they beleeue his words of whom MOSES wrote, These Bookes shall accuse them, the witnesses which God the Father beareth of his Sonne; The other Booke is the Booke of Life, written with the names of Saints that shall liue for ever; To whom the iust Iudge shall deliver the possession of that Kingdome that shall never passe away to be destroyed, but remaineth for ever, even for ever and ever.

The foule Beast, some of his purtenances will be wanting if his hornes be not farther Considered; foure came vp out of the North part of his head, the French Emperours; of the South side sixe Spanish; before whom, there were Three of the first, their Race pluckt vp by the Rootes; amongst these came vp an other little Horne about the midst of the time: in this Horne were eyes, like the eyes of a man, in workmanship striuing to set Nature a patterne; curious in all Arts, and doing honour to vertue, but wanting the gift of grace, opened a fearefull Mouth; the King of the East, whose looke is more stout then the highest of his fellow Hornes.

Hitherto is the end of the matter of these earthly Monarchies, and the day of Iudgement hath beene also declared the matter of the end: The Story is yet but chalked out, Therefore in these following Visions is contained more at large, the occurrence of those dayes before mentioned, even to the end of the world; Wherein my desire is, not as hee that rowleth a stone to returne vpon himselfe, but to make it a twisted Threefold Cord, to draw vp the weight that presseth so hard of infidelitie.

The Prophet beheld till the auncient of dayes did sit to Iudge the quicke and the dead, and the Beast cast aliue into the Lake Fire, his Body destroyed and given to the Burning flame, to be tormented day and night, for ever and ever.

DANIEL. Chap. VIII.

IN the third yeare of Belshazzer a Vision appeared vnto Daniel alone, even to himselfe, and hee heard a mans voyce that called, saying; Gabriel, make the man vnderstand the Vision; so he came neere vnto him, and said; O Sonne of man; the time of this Vision extends to the end of all things; behold therefore I will make thee know what shall come to passe, euen to the last day, the great day of Wrath and Indignation, for at the time appointed the end ſhall be.

Medes and Persians } The rovghe Goate. }	{ Send mee Spaniards { The Gothe roagve.

The firſt matter giuen him to vnderſtand, is the breaking in peeces of the Roman Empire, which ſpiritually is called *Sodome* and *Egipt*; where alſo the members of our Lords Body are Crucified, ſignified by the Ram, the Hee Goate is the *Turke*; The *Roman* Emperours the Two hornes in the Eaſt and Weſt, are alſo ſignified by the Kings of *Media* and *Perſia*. The foure Kingdomes ſtanding vp out of that Nation, are the Iſles of Great *Britaine*, *France*, *Spaine*, and *Turky*.

Laſtly, the Goate himſelfe ſhall be hunted by a King of a fierce Countenance, not regarding the perſon of the old, nor ſhewing fauour to the young, caſting downe ſome of the hoaſt of Pharoah, and of the Starres to the ground : For the tranſgreſſion againſt the daily Sacrifice was the Hoaſt given over : A King vnderſtanding darke ſentences which are ſome part of the holy Scriptures, through policie and supposed wisdome, he shall cause the craft of the Divell to prosper, for by Peace and affected pittie, and satisfying the ambitious mindes of some Christians, he shall not only draw them to denie the faith, but many others following their example: Not by his owne power, but by the Divells policie he shall be mighty, whose looke is more stout then his fellowes, But by the great day of the Lord, he shall be broken without hand.

Now in those dayes, when the Goate was come close vnto the Ramme, and had cast him downe and stamped vpon him; The Prophet that beheld as by a perspectiue these remote things, heard also one Saint speaking, and an other Saint said vnto that certaine Saint that spoke, how long is the time from this Vision to the end of the world, that the holy Citie of God, and his chosen People be no longer trodden vnder foote; And hee said vnto mee vnto Two Thousand Three hundred dayes; Then shall the Sanctuarie bee cleansed, and the holy People Iustified.

The dayes bee so many yeares to the end of the world, beginning at the Vision, which was about the yeare of the world, 3425.

Of the certaine Saints speaking, or the nomber of wonderfull secrets, I omit to speake, that to the most part might appeare (being in this Land, and these late dayes) but some tale of a Phenix, though to bee testified of more then fiue hundred men and women besides my selfe.

DANIEL. CHAP. IX.

AFter these Visions in the first yeare of DARIVS the Son of AHASHVERVS, the Prophet vnderstood by Bookes and Computations, the nomber of yeares whereof the word of the Lord came to IEREMIAH the Prophet, concerning the desolation of *Ierusalem*, that seventie yeares should be accomplished; And whilst hee was speaking in Prayer, and presenting his supplication before the Lord for the holy

Mountaine the People of God, euen for the holy Citie the Church, that to the end of the world must be trodden vnder foote, whereof that ruinons place the Citie of *Ierusalem*, is a figure trodden downe at this day. Yet was this *Hebron* built seaven yeares before *Zoan* in *Egipt*.

The man GABRIEL which was caused to flie swiftly, touched him and said (alluding to the former matter of his studie and meditations, as of troublous, appetites, and Cogitations somtimes Dreames are deriued) O DANIEL: I am come vnto thee againe to giue thee more skill and vnderstanding; Seuentie weekes are determined vpon the holy Citie, signifying the time, not onely when the Sonne of God by his suffering should make reconciliation for sinne, but a time and times and part of time, three dayes and a halfe, halfe the mysticall Weeke, to make an end of Sinnes to finish transgression, and to make a new Heaven and a new Earth, wherein dwelleth everlasting righteousnesse to seale vp the Visions and Prophecies with the Seale of assurance, that all these things are past and true, and to annoint the most holy King and Kings, and Lord and Lords, the first and the last.

And here againe the Angell GABRIEL willeth him to know and vnderstand the things of which he shall informe him; The first is this, that from the going forth of the Commandement, which is the beginning of the Creation to the building of the new Ierusalem, the second comming of *Messiah* the Prince the Sonne of God, it shall be Seaven Weekes or Seaven Moneths, as it is spoken by EZEKIEL the Prophet; Then the desolate Citie the Sanctuary shall be walled in, in a troublous time, to make a seperation betweene the Sanctuary and the Prophane place.

And in the middest of this Propheticall weeke, after Threescore and Two weekes, *Messiah* shalbe cut off, the Son of God shalbe Crucified and be deliuered vnto the *Gentiles*, & they shal scourge him & put him to death; the People of the Prince (for it was not lawfull for the *Iewes* to put any man to Death) these People the *Roman* Nation shall destroy the Citie of *Ierusalem* and the Sanctuary, at the end of which Warre there ſhall begin a floud of Fyre (kindled in our Saviours dayes) during the Raigne of thoſe Ethnick Beares, and the abomination of deſolation ſtanding where it ought not; then let him that is in *Iudea* flye to the wilde Mountaines for ſafety; for in thoſe times Iudgement did begin at the houſe of God; and if firſt Iuſtice did begin at his Children and Servants in this life, what ſhall the end bee of his Enemies, whom hee hates in the world to come, that haue not obeyed the Goſpell of God.

Theſe Flouds the Serpent will caſt out of his Mouth, a time and times & halfe a Time, to trie them of the holy Covenant, their boldneſſe, what confidence they haue concerning the Lords oath, and whether they will perſeuer in this holineſſe and righteouſneſſe all their dayes to their liues end, and not rather feare his power, who is Sathan the Prince of this world, or at leaſt the furious cruell hands of his torturing Inſtruments.

Whose liues cannot satisfie their malice; for had not the senselesse earth shewed more pitty then they, opening her Mouth to helpe these poore outcasts, their torments had beene endlesse; Sooner they may swim, and sinke in their Blood, then daunt or foyle their courage, not abashed for their Boasts, threats, nor fiery Brands they feare them not at all; their Triumphs are graven vpon the Palmes of the Lords hands, hee forgets them no more, then a Mother forgets her new-borne Sonne, her sucking childe, when the Tongue cleaues to the roofe of the Mouth for Thirst, to haue compassion on him; be of good cheere, you haue peace in Christ, though tribulation in this world; persecutions are but like the Trauell of a Woman, who hath sorrow because her houre is come, but as soone as shee is delivered of the Childe, shee remembreth no more the anguish, for ioy a man-childe is borne into the world.

The Lambe, the Bread of life shall feede them, they shall hunger nor thirst no more, hee shall wipe all Teares from the eyes of his

Children; these vilde Bodyes, subiect to all infirmities, shall then be made like his owne glorified Body, of more perfection then our first Parents, a living Soule that shall not dye to Sinne; neither shall the heate of the Sunne smite them; for hee shall haue mercy vpon them, and leade them to liuing Fountaines of truth, cleere as Christall; these that come to him, or overcome the world, hunger no more, they haue rest and peace for paine, and by their white Robes and Palmes in their hands, the Ensignes of peace and victorie; they shall be knowne, neither to be Heretiques or Schismatiques, but his servants that haue fought for his Kingdome that it should not be delivered vp vnto Antichrist.

The followers of him, who shall shortly tread these Traitors in the great Wine-presse of the wrath of God, who haue turned away their Eares from the wholsome Scriptures, the Leaues of which are for the healing of the Nations, that they might be rubbed with the Prophane fables of Drunken doting old wiues.

But with all the faithfull the Lord ſhall confirme his truth and Covenant for a Weeke from the beginning of the world vntill the laſt end therof; This week is Seven thouſand yeares, conſiſting of yeares, Moneths and weekes; finiſhed when the Kingdomes of this world, are become the Kingdomes of our Lord, and of his Chriſt, and hee ſhall Raigne for ever and ever: When the Tenth part of the Citie fell, the Tenne dayes of Tribulation are ended; Seven thouſand names of men ſlaine in the great Earthquake, *Dies Solis; Dies Lunæ, Dies Martis, Dies Mercurij; Dies Iovis, Dies Veneris, Dies Saturni;* the remnant were affrighted; and gaue glory vnto the God of Heaven.

For wee muſt not be ignorant of this one thing, that one day with the Lord is as a Thouſand yeare, and a Thouſand yeare as one day; In the middeſt of which Weeke, the Lord ſhall cauſe the oblation and Sacrifice to ceaſe, ſaying, Sacrifice and Offering thou wouldeſt not, but a Body haſt thou prepared mee without ſpot, for the redemption of the tranſgreſſions that were vnder the firſt Teſtament. The Blood of which firſt Teſtament of Beaſts, God enioyned to purifie the patternes of heavenly things, the Veſſels of the Miniſtrie, but the heavenly things themſelues with better Sacrifices (which are the Conſciences to purge them from dead workes, that they may be cleane veſſels to ſerue the living God.)

Thus hee once ſuffered, the vncreated in likeneſſe of a Creature like feeble ſinfull fleſh, ſowne in weakeneſſe and diſhonour in the Duſt, but raiſed in Power & the Brightneſſe of his Fathers Glory, the expreſſe Image of his perſon, over whoſe excellent Nature, voyd of violence and deceit, the Graue could get no victory, no more then the wombe can keepe backe a ſonne at the time of perfection, redeemed from the Bowels of the Earth, and ranſomed by the riches of his owne vnſearchable Treaſure and quickning Spirit.

This ſeeming vgly Serpent, rather ſome ſhadow or his skin, at whoſe approach men turne pale and quake more terrified then hurt; But rocking Babes the faithfull a sleepe, others run raving with staring frenzie for feare, as if this once appointed so were fits to be chased away, not calling to minde the Resurrection of IESVS CHRIST, hath opened his Iawes, his Sting cut out and nayled to the Crosse, that bold Champion scorning to be his executioner, setting his victorious foot vpon the Traytors head, by spirituall alliance kinne to the Divell, proud of advantage, bites the Heele of our Saviour with his rotten Teeth, for want of his Poysoned sting.

But heare ô Death vnstop thine Adders eares from whose Mole-sighted eyes, the light of Repentance is hid, behold thy time and Plague is at hand; thy pined crying Prisoners, thou shall restraine their libertie no longer, that say our Bones are dryed and our hope is lost, when shall we dwell in the Land of the living; behold, thy Caues and Castles shall be destroyed & broken downe, and the Earth that opened her Mouth and swallowed vp the Flood shall cast it vp againe in the twinkling of an Eye, thou shalt giue vp thy accompts, for of the Sonnes and

Daughters of the Lord, thou ſhalt not keepe backe ſo much as the leaſt, whoſe names are written in the Booke of life.

And laſtly, Viper, ſeed of the olde Serpent, thy ſentence is for that bold attempt; Fuller of malice then hurt, thy houſe ſhall be burned with vnquenchable Fire, the Place ſowne with vnſauory poyſoned Salt, and thy Carrion-carkaſſe ſwallowed vp of thine owne Brood the ſecond Death.

All which myſticall Weeke or Seaven Moneths formerly mentioned, as it is ſpoken by the Prophet EZECHIEL; The Land of *Iſraell* ſhalbe burying of *Gog* that Sathan, that the Land may be cleanſed.

Hitherto are the matters talked of between the man GABRIEL and the Prophet.

DANIEL. CHAP. X.

IN the third yeare of CYRUS King of *Perſia*, a thing was revealed to DANIEL (whoſe name was called BELTESHAZZER) and the thing was true but the time appointed was long. These are the things not only come to passe, in this latter age of the world, but at this time and in this day; signified by the Son of God to the Prophet.

Prince of Persia.— I can Pope Friers.

Divell. *I can Pope Friers. Man hold vp my Traine?*
Pope. *Kings I Depose, and all their Race, to Raigne.*
Divell. *And Popes to Friers I can turne againe.*

The Prince of the Kingdome of *Persia*, (that Lord by whom the Lord of Lords was withstood,) is Sathan the Divell, Michael one of the first Princes that came then to helpe him; This is Iames King of Great *Britaine*, and the man who is raised on high: The one and Twenty dayes; the Lord making no forfeiture, are so many Hundred yeares, beginning at the Vision, and ending this present, 1600. And so long the words of this Vision haue been closed & sealed vp; Even till now the time of the end.

This most Blessed person the Saviour of the world, remained with the Kings of *Persia*, the *Roman* Emperors (signified so vnto DANIEL being the present Monarchy) till there arose vp a new King in *Egipt* which knew not IOSEPH, and said vnto his People; Behold, the People of the Children of *Israell* are more, and mightier then wee, Therfore set over thē Taskmasters to afflict them with Burthens, but the more they did afflict them, the more they multiplied and grew. These Kings placed in the highest Thrones, to walke in his Statutes to execute his Iudgements, but because they gaue more Eare, and harkened rather to false Prophets then to ELIAS and MOSES, for severitie and meeknesse; Representing the Law and the Gospell, suffering their Bodies to lye dead in the streets in an vnknowne Tongue, even hee the Lord departed from them; and with the sword of his Mouth will fight with their Prince Sathan, renewing alwayes his old quarrell against the Church of God.

And here these Kings forsaken of IESVS CHRIST, for one secret friend which is the Divell, they haue two open Enemies, the *Turke* and the *Pope*, making their Crownes his footstoole, this did not CÆSAR, by these Three the Empire being devided; what can remaine but the bare Image; or the Image of the Picture of him, whose deadly wound was healed: Bearing at this day, as Thunder goes before Lightning, for their fatall device, the sad Fowle blazoned with the ominous Colours of the blacke Horse; for feare, but halfe displaying her wings, in stead of her beake, shee casts her heads, the Eagle hath Mued her Feathers; Though thou exalt thy selfe as the Eagle, and though thou set thy neast amongst the Starres, thence will I bring thee downe saith the Lord.

These things hitherto mentioned concerning the last Vision is the preamble for this that followeth, for here the Sonne of God whose eyes were like a flame of fire; and his feet like fine brasse, saith he will shew vnto the man greatly beloued, that which is noted in the Scripture of truth, which is the *Reuelation*, the sayings of which are faithfull and true, that there is none, or but one, that holdeth with him in these things, which is the true Interpretation of the Scripture, but MICHAEL our Prince of Great *Britaine* and *Ireland*, that fights and contends with the Enemies of the Lord, about his Body, disputing with them, haue transubstantiated & changed the truth of God into a lye, worshipping and serving the Creature more then the Creator, for which cause God gaue them vp, &c.

Now followeth that that is noted in the Scripture of that Prince. After the Temple of God was opened in Heaven, wherein was seene the Arke of his Testament, overlaid round about with gold, wherein was the golden Pot that had Manna, and ARONS Rodde that budded, and the Tables of the Covenant, And over it the Cherubins of glory, covering the Mercy-Seate, and Lightnings and voyces, and Thunders, &c. This is the Millitant Church that brought foorth the Man-childe, the word of God, caught vp vnto God, and to his Throne, after which the Woman fled into the Wildernesse, where shee was fed A thousand two hundred and threescore dayes, which are so many yeares.

The first accompt beginneth from the destruction of *Ierusalem*, when the abomination of desolation, did stand in the Holy place, the yeares being the same spoken in the last Vision of the Prophet DANIEL, though thirty yeares be taken away, because the Court without the Temple was left out, given vnto the Gentiles, for the Raigne of the first Christian Emperour.

These yeares doe reach to the dayes of those blessed Men; when the light of the Gospell did first begin to shine, after the great Mist, lasting a Thousand two hundred and ninetie yeares, dayes of darknesse and gloominesse of Cloudes, and thicke Mists, when the third part of the Sunne was smitten, and the third part of the Moone, and the third part of the Starres, which are innumerable; After these dayes were past, there was warre in Heaven, MICHAEL and his Angells, fought against the Dragon, and the Dragon fought, and his Angells the Iesuites, and prevailed not, neither was their place found any more in Heaven.

Heaven is here taken in this place for the

Church of God, the fray is fought by seconds, by MICHAEL is meant King IAMES; The Dragon needs little exposition, It is the Pope, for MICHAEL overcame by the blood of the Lambe, and by the testimony of so many Bishops, and other faithfull, crowned with the Glory of Martyrdome; Therefore reioyce yee Church of God, yee Congregations of the faithfull, and ye Professors that dwell amongst them, and woe to the Earth and to the Sea, the Congregation of that Sinagogue the Sea of *Rome*, Sathans seate, where Sathan dwelleth, for the Pope, the Dragon, the Divell is amongst you, having great wrath, because he knoweth he hath but a short time, two woes are past, and behold the third woe commeth shortly.

Blessed are the Dead that dye in the Lord, for they rest from their labours, and their works follow them, and this is the truth noted in the Scripture of Truth, of MICHAEL, And God make the name and Throne, of the King his Sonne, better, and greater then his.

Though I owe no defence for the name of an Angell given to a Mortall man (in this Prophesie) yet to satisfie as well the Envious as the Ignorant, they shall finde the Sonne of God sometimes called by the name of the first Adam, David who shall feede his Flocke like a Shepheard, and gather his Lambes with his arme, and carry them in his bosome, stiled a man after Gods owne Hart; and in another place from his owne Mouth, holding it no derogation to his Divine Nature, to apply to himselfe by Parables the properties of an austere Master, a Cruell vsurer, or the vniust Iudge, May by the same Authoritie giue the name of Michael, or like vnto God in some respects vnto this Prince who fought the battell of the Lord, more like an Angell then a Mortall Man; as to the other the name of Dragon, because he spake as a Dragon.

As this young Dragon hath acted his part, his Syer or Damme the old Dragon, his markes may not be forgotten, whose Hornes haue beene formerly mentioned in a Miter and Diadem, his seaven Heads are so many

Rulers, as it were Husbands or ſeverall ſorts of Magiſtracy, governing that Common-wealth, and the ſeaven Crownes are ſeaven Hundreth yeares, beeing the time from *Romes* foundation to the firſt Emperour. *Equæua polo*, *Eterna, Antiqua, Caput Mundi, Celſa. Deum locus. Cœleſtis.* Names of Blaſphemie.

DANIEL. Chap. XI.

Darius the Med. — I Dreamed thus.

BEſides this Prince of victorious and bleſſed memory, who came to helpe the King of Kings, that ſate vpon the white Horſe, whoſe name is the word of God, to fight the Battell in Heaven againſt the Prince of the Kingdome of *Perſia*, here is an other of like happy memory, that hath the Honour to haue his name Recorded in this holy antient Prophecie, Constantine the Great, named, Darius the *Mede*, raigning thirtie yeares. In the firſt times of which renowmed Monarchy the Lord ſtood to confirme and ſtrengthen him. After whoſe time three Kings ſtood vp together in *Perſia*, dividing the Empire, which breach, made way for the fourth, the fourth Beaſt, corrupted with Riches and libertie; Farre richer then they all, By whoſe ſtrength through his riches, Christian Princes were ſtirred vp againſt Mahomet, growing not a little great by their ruines.

And a mighty King ſhall ſtand vp, the great King of *Tyre*, the abſolute Monarch thereof, and all the dependences Northward, that ſhall rule with great dominion, and doe according to his owne will, and when hee ſhall ſtand vp the fundamentall Lawes of his Kingdome ſhall bee broken and infringed; And the Kingdome ſhall be divided towards the foure windes of Heaven, and not to his poſterity, nor according to his Dominion which hee ruled, for this Kingdome ſhall be pluckt vp, even for others, beſides thoſe that were planted therein; his naturall ſubiects by a diſpenſation being freed from their oath of obedience.

Caroli Magni Christianissimi Romanorum Imperatoris
Corpus hoc conditum est sepulchro.

After this the King of the South was strong, and he was strong aboue the King of the North, and he had dominion, and his Dominion is a great dominion.

These two Kings, the King of the North, and the King of the South parting the ten Hornes, the Princes of *Tyre* and *Ethiopia*; In the end of yeares they shall ioyne themselues together, for the Kings Daughter of the South shall come to the King of the North to make an agreement, but shee shall not retaine the power of the Arme, neither shall he stand nor his Arme, or they shall be Childlesse, and she shall be given vp, And they that brought her sent away destitute of a Father, and forsaken of her Brother.

But out of a branch of her rootes, which are her Father and her Mother, signifying their Incestuous Mariages, One shall stand vp in his Estate very hardy, and shall come with an Armie, and shall enter into the fortresse of the King of the North; or the King of *Tyre*, and deale against them and prevaile; And shall carry Captiues into *Egipt*, their Gods and their Prnices, and with their Pretious Vessells of Silver and Gold, and hee shall continue more yeares then the King of the North in the Monarchy; So the King of the South, or the King of *Ethiopia* shall returne into his owne Land, the Land of Dust and Ashes, where his worst Enemies doe not envie his quiet possession: But his Sonnes who succeeded each other in the Monarchy, shall be stirred vp against the King of the North, and shall assemble a great multitude of Forces, and one of them shall certainly come and overflow with a floud of Fury, and shall passe through, and prevaile against them of the Holy Covenant; But after that hee shall returne and be stirred vp, even to his Fortresse or best Fenced place by them.

And the King of the South, or one of these Brothers shall be provoked with Choller, and shall come forth and fight with the King of the North, who shall set forth a great multitude, but the multitude ſhall bee given into the hands of his Enemies, and himſelfe ſhall be his Priſoner carried a Captiue into *Ethiopia*.

And when the King of the South, or this *Perſian* King hath taken away the multitude, his heart ſhall be lifted vp againſt God; and he ſhall caſt downe many of his ſervants Tenne Thouſands; but neither hee nor thoſe that come after ſhall bee ſtrengthened thereby.

(For at the end of Yeares, which are now expired, there ſhall certainely come a King of the North, and hee ſhall ſet forth a multitude greater then the former, a great Army and with much riches, and hee ſhall doe according to his owne will, &c.)

And in thoſe former dayes there ſhall many ſtand vp againſt the King of the South; alſo the Robbers of the Chriſtians, theſe Extortioners ſhall exalt themſelues, to eſtabliſh the Viſion of the Prophets, and the Figures of the Law, which Prophecied vntill IOHN; for the firſt things that are but ſhadowes, are now vaniſhed away, to establish the second, but they shall fall, So the King of the North shall come and cast vp a Mount, and take the most fenced Cities; and the Armes of the South shall not withstand, neither his chosen People, neither shall there bee any strength to withstand, But hee that commeth against him, shall doe according to his owne will, and none shall stand before him; and hee shall stand in the glorious Land which by him shall be consumed, Hee shall also set his face to enter with the strength of his whole Kingdome, and vpright ones with him; thus shall hee doe.

And hee shall giue him the Daughter of Women, or a Queene by decent, whose Royall blood was corrupted, and stayned by the vsurping authority of a Tyranous Husband, but she shall not stand on his side, neither before him, for hee dying shee was brought home, and shortly after Married to another,

After which agreement dissolued, and the League broken, his Successor shall turne his face vnto the *Brittish* Iles, and shall take many Prisoners, but a Prince for his owne behalfe, rather then the honour of God of a happy daring shall cause the reproach offered to cease without his owne reproach, hee caused the shame to turne vpon him that opposeth and exalteth himselfe aboue all that is called God. The Lord sometimes prouiding the remedy before the sore, as carefull Physitians haue Drugs in store for all diseases, preparing the disobedience of VASTHI, and the vnlawfull diuorce, for the preseruation of the *Iewes*, to hang proud HAMMON and all his wicked Sonnes, so this Prince throwing vnder foote his Cappe of Maintenance (whose visage was vnmask'd, by a Munke not long before) those *Babel* Monasteries, vnmeete Cages for such Craignes, Ostriges, and chanting Owles, digesting not only all the thorney-Choaking Heresie of false Prophets, but the rusty Purgatory fictions of Heathen Poets, The doings of these vncleane and hatefull birds, Though as the eating of doung I loathe them in my Mouth, yet since our Sauiour and Lord himselfe vouchsafed to cast his

Eye towards those secret privie places, bidding vs take heed of their Deserts, I may not stop my Nose or Mouth for nicenesse, but rather thinke it my part to empty such houses of office, if weakenesse did not prevent and hinder my willingnesse.

Yet with mine owne hand according to my might (God willing) I will throw one stone at this *Thracian* Witch, the wicked Prophet; If I cannot breake his head, I will breake his Harpe if I can, before lies passe headlong downe to Hell the streame: Neither will omit her Holinesse (though her natiue Soile and Sex may challenge some fauour) how they shall walke then, Inseparably hand in hand togither; And as certaine of their owne Poets mention, her vntimely Death, stung by the false Scorpion, that lurk'd so close in the grasse, of his gamesome villany.

This Beast (or rather Divell) for so hee seemes by his description, by the stamping of his Oxe feete. Long teeth of Iron, nayles of Brasse, and ten Hornes, or at least some horrible Monster in his likenesse, takes vpon

him

him to giue, by his Marke to all the world most cursed Dispensations: To please Herod it shall be lawfull to Marry his Daughter to her Husbands owne Brother, the Vncle to his Neece: Thus vnnaturall he is not satisfied in most prodigious manner to abuse himselfe, but others must doe Incestuously by his Example. These vomited things, are now savory meate, neither can Sathan, cast out Sathan: Then it is granted they can Erre, which Cunning lesson had he not learned of his lying Father, his Kingdome long since, had beene divided and broken in pieces. Bee it never so vnlawfull, like the Law of the *Medes* and *Persians*, the Decree may not be changed.

Thus out of the sentences of the holy Scripture, this Spider sucks somtimes his poyson, saying in his Hart, All the Kingdoms of the "Earth are mine, My Father the Divell hath "given them vnto me, and rather of my E- "state then abate a button; I will teach men "as many lyes to damne them, as wee can "both inuent, that with the breath of my "Mouth I blow in and out the fire of Pur-

"gatory, where People beleeue some Soules "are blood-raw, others rosted to death, that "I make the Creator, sacrifice and sell their "Saviour, which puts me in minde of *Iudas* "my Brother, whose hanging I could hear-"tily lament, had hee not like a passionate "foole, so ill playd his last part.

" Admit of his weaknesse he did repent, is "a wise man the Trumpet of his owne "shame? to say he had Err'd to be his owne "accuser, what did he gaine by this; some "say forsooth, This Confession of friends "and foes, might be, to leaue the subtill El-"ders, and their generation the *Iewes*, with-"out excuse, though wee eate both of one "Sop, I like not the Example, I meane the "manner; It is olde and weake, and lame "Arguments will follow fast enough; Idle "Confessions, are no secrets to me, I like not "his tragicall speech, it was timorous, had "it beene by boasting, scoffing, or to ad-"vance his service, as it proued earnest, more "might bee said in his defence. I doe the "same my-selfe: but let it passe, my plot was "no pen to blot his name, and had it pre-

" vailed, the fire is witnesse, his frailtie had " never flowne so farre.

" When I call to minde my predecessors, " no small puffe can blow my pride downe, " shall I degenerate, or not follow their " steps, IUDAS the Apostle, and IULIA-" NUS the Emperour, no Ring-leaders of " that Nazaren poore Sect, that leave the " certaine Blisse of this world, to beleeue " Scripture promises made to the Fathers " had I beene in their dayes, though they " were couragious, both faithlesse, and false " enough, I can lift my heele as high as " theirs, I had gone before them in their " owne craft.

" Yet since it was not remorce of Consci-" ence, but the vngratefull answer of the " chiefe Priests, and all his hopes frustrate, " this cast the Man away, my Pardon as be-" neficiall to him as to others, shall cost him " nothing, this accident vpon that ill advi-" sed answer: WHAT IS THAT TO " US LOOKE THOU TO THAT, was the " first motiue that made me coine Absoluti-" on, which passeth now for currant Silver, "being all the Fees the deſperate Traitors "get of mee towards their hanging, this "ditch-water I giue the poore ſoules for A- "qua vitæ, when they goe to the Gallowes.

If ſome will ſay this ſtone is caſt too far, I ſay but a Dreame of like, or leſſe horror, would haue ſtarted, or as throughly awakened themſelues to behold ſo great a Tyrant, a Prince ſo gratious & good, his Kingdome with ſo much pride, and ſpitefully invaded; All his naturall Subiects become diſobedient Rebells, except a Remnant of ſome few, forſaking their liues, that lou'd not their liues to the Second Death, ſuffering for their loyalty & loue vnexpreſſable, fiery exquiſite bloody torments, his Cittizens amongſt whom hee Inhabited, with one voyce Crying out all at once. Away with this Man, ſaying, we will not haue this Man to raigne over vs, himſelfe (ô gentle Doue) dumbe as a Sheepe before the ſheerer, hanged by the hands as an off-ſcouring, ſet vp like a Marke for an Arrow, reviled, made a deriſion, as their Muſicke; to his People, ſweating drops of blood downe to the ground, the barres of sorrow preventing the passage of Teares, (all in vaine) in so strong an Agony, more for griefe and anguish of them and their Children? then his owne feare, of those vnspeakable paines and torments, Crying with a lowde voice, vnable to conceale that passion, MY GOD, MY GOD, VVHY HAST THOU FORSAKEN MEE, my tongue cleaveth to my jawes, thou hast brought me into the dust of death through his tender Mercy, shedding from his pierced side, blood from the wound, for a sensible Testimony of a true Sacrifice, and water to Baptise and wash them, whose hard hearts could not weepe for themselues. He wiste the Spirit of the Lord, was departed from him.

Stones rent, the Earth quaking, not Ghosts walking, but Graues opening, and dead Bodyes amazed, and awaking, The whole Globe Mourning in Sable blacknesse, except Man, at the dreadfull Funerall of this most mighty Prince; The Sonne as Chiefe, covering and hiding his astonished face, with hideous Cloudes, as blacke as Sackcloth of haire, to vtter the height and depth of silent speaking sorrow, by whose darke vaile and traine the shadow of Death, turning the Day to Night, wherein all Creatures are a Corps, and the world but a Tombe, detesting and abhorring his Beames of light should beare witnesse, the true light of Men, by mankinde was so vngratefully and vnkindely extinguished, the expresse Pure Image of the Maker, the Prince of life, The Person of God, (not made) turn'd to a lumpe of Clay, by a shamelesse accusation, an vnjust sentence, and a cursed Executoner. To Slay these Lords that haue dominion over vs, hee pulled the house downe vpon his owne head, the mightie deliverer of *Israel*.

His God head and death being Incompatible, choosing rather to forgoe, and forsake the one, then forget his promise, leaue the will of his Father vndone, or his worke vnfinished; His sufferings being by a vacancy of Power, as sometimes cold, may abate and abolish the sense of feeling, yet retayned by the vitall parts, the losse is not irrecoverable.

Whose Hart would not melt, Haire stare,

and Hands become faint, to write or heare such a story.

Yet here is not an end, what shall he doe, now chased as a Bird betweene Heaven and Earth since his resurrection, pull'd by Bitts to peeces, throwne to hungry Hell-hounds, the Divells Dogs, Caniballs; did not his power to deliver his Darling, surmount the greedy arrogant policie of these *Barbarians*; spoken without aggravation both one Spaune, acting (in their Copes, I might say, party coloured fooles Coates) like painted Peacocks, the part of HECUBA, the franticke Troyan Wiues and POLLIXINA, Such pompe and gaudinesse of Masking garments, being fitter for the Theator then the Temple, the state thereof requiring rather Mourners with all their BACCUS Savage Ceremonies, apish and affected Fashions, No Vice on a Stage, with senselesse jests to move the vulgars laughter, good folkes ashamed; So rediculous, without vnderstanding babling like Parrots or Children, a Tongue they know not; yet no Babes or Children in Mallice, Pyping without distinction; Pricketh not this the hearts of the hearers, twanging vpon a Harpe, Instead of an Egge, asking a Scorpion ; and saying *Amen* to any *Pater-Nester*.

Is there any sorrow like this, whose Mirth is so great ; whose heart so hard , as not to be greeved for this affliction ; can wee forbeare to bow our selues, and not to Travell for these paines ; To heare the Arke not only is taken, but helpe Lord alas, to see the Heire apparant of the living God so dishonoured and mangled amongst his Enemies! O the wonder of wonders, a lying Wonder, to see creatures endued with sense and reason, beleeue a senslesse Miracle ; here is the Doctrine or spirits of Divells, three uncleane spirits, Three Frogs forg'd one like another, or a false lye spit vp by the Divell, the Beast, and the false Prophet from their vncleane slimy Mouthes, Into the Ovens and kneading Troughs of the Kings of the Earth, and of the whole world, to gather them to the Battell of the great Day of God Almighty ; Also to decide the question) with full consent) when this doctrine working miracles was coniured vp. When Transgressors are come to the full; the water dried vp, that the way of the Kings of the East might bee prepared; The *Tartars* whose looke is more stout then his fellowes. Righteous art thou ô Lord, which art, which wast, and shall be, because thou hast iudged thus; for they haue shed the Blood of Saints and Prophets; and thou hast given them vp to blaspheme the God of Heaven, to beleeue a lye, false teachers that teach, thou hast given them Blood to drinke, the Blood of the living God, as it were the Blood of a Dead man, here is a sore lye, a grievous Soare, well may such mad Dogs gnaw their Blistered Tongues.

Then shall stand vp in his estate, a raiser of Taxes in the glory of the Kingdome; but in few dayes hee shall bee destroyed in the strength of his Age, neither in anger, nor in Battaile, but in a sport of Tilting by a splinter in his Eye.

And in his estate shall stand vp a vilde person, or a Luxurious, to whom they shall not giue the honour of the Kingdome, but he ſhall come in peaceably and obtayne the Kingdome by Flatterie; and with the Armes of a Flood, or as the ſodaine inundation of *Nilus*; ſo ſhall the Faithfull people be over-flowne from before him, they ſhall bee broken by a cruell Maſſacre, yea, alſo the Prince of the Covenant, and after the league made with him, even the Great King of the North, hee ſhall worke deceitfully with the holy people; for hee ſhall come vp and ſhall become ſtrong with a ſmall people, he ſhall enter peaceably even vpon the fatteſt places of the Province, for he ſhall doe that which his Fathers haue not done, nor his Fathers Fathers, he ſhall ſcatter among them the prey, ſpoyle and riches of the wicked; yea, and he ſhall fore-caſt his devices againſt the ſtrong Holds of Sathan for a time, not to the End; And he ſhall ſtir vp his Power and his great Courage againſt the King of the South with a great Army, & the King of the South ſhall be ſtirred vp to Battell with a very great and mightie Army, but hee ſhall not ſtand for they ſhall fore-caſt devices againſt him; yea, his owne Dogs (ſtiled Gods) that feed of the Portion of his meate ſhall deſtroy him.

After whoſe deceaſe his Army ſhall overflow, and many of the righteous ſhall fall downe ſlaine, and both theſe Kings hearts ſhalbe to doe miſchiefe, and they ſhall ſpeake lies againſt the knowne truth, both at one Table, but it ſhall not proſper; for yet the end of all things ſhall be at the time appointed, Then ſhall hee returne into his owne Land with great riches, and little profit; and his hart ſhall be againſt the holy Covenant; therefore the next blow was at the hart. And he ſhall doe exploits, and returne to his own Land.

At the time appointed, hee ſhall returne even the King of the North ſpoken of before, that ſhould certainly come after certaine yeares with a great Army, and a multitude greater then the former with much riches, and ſhall come towards the South, but it ſhal not be as the former, or as the latter; for hee ſhall wound as it were his owne ſides. The Ships of Shittim ſhall come againſt him; therefore he ſhall be grieved and returne againſt his owne ſtrength, and haue indignation againſt the holy Covenants; So he ſhall doe; he ſhall returne, and haue intelligence with them that forſake the holy Covenant; theſe Ships built with pretious Wood, whoſe Anchor is the Lord, toſſed too and fro with floudes of vngodly men in the Sea of *Babilon*, and compaſſed with the Waues of Death; but when they cry vnto the Lord, and are at their wits end. Hee who walketh vpon the Sea, draweth nigh vnto them, and bringeth them out of their diſtreſſe; hee maketh the ſtorme a calme, as a Childe, even ſo ſuddenly he ſtilleth the roaring Waues of this Tempeſtious Sea, lifted vp with the ſtormy windes of Sathans malice.

Therefore thus ſaith the Lord vnto *Tyrus*, O thou that art Scituate at the entry of the Sea; which art a Merchant for the People for many Iſles. Thus ſaith the Lord God; O *Tyrus* thou haſt ſaid, I am a perfect beautie. Thy Borders are in the midſt of the Seas, thy buildings haue perfected thy beautie; they haue made all thy Ship Boords all of Firre Trees of Senir; they haue taken Cedars from *Libanan*, to make Maſts for thee; of the Okes of *Basban* haue they made thine Oares; the Company of the *Asburites* haue made thy Benches of Ivorie, brought out of the Isles of *Chittim*; Fyne Linnen with broydered worke from *Egipt*, was that which thou spreadest forth to bee thy Sayle, Blew and Purple from the Isles of ELISHAH, was that which covered thee, &c.

And Armies of the vngodly shall stand on his part; they shall pollute the Sanctuary of strength, and shall take away the daily Sacrifice, and shall place therein the abomination, that maketh the house of God desolate, turning it into a Den of Theeues (the daily Sacrifice, or the Lords Supper shall be taken away to place the Divells Idoll, the Supper of the Lord, instituted in remembrance of our Redemption, as the Passeover was a Commemoration that the Lord passed over the houses of the Children of *Israel* in *Egipt*, when hee smote the *Egiptians* and delivered them. DAVID a man after Gods own heart, poured out vnto the Lord, the Water of *Bethlem*, that he so sore longed to drinke, the blood of Mortall men, that went in jeopardy of their liues, yet damned people are told they drinke of God our Lord IESUS CHRIST his heart-blood. Shewing themselues more thirsty after it, then the greedy *Iewes*, these blood-suckers will haue it before his side be pierced.

And such as doe wickedly against the Covenant, to breake the Commandements of God, the vow, vowed in their Baptisme, by which they forsake the Divell; with all the Covetous and Carnall desires of the flesh; these vncleane vilde persons shall be corrupted by flatteries, and easily drawne from the truth, to beleeue a lye, that they may bee damned, that hath pleasure in vnrighteousnesse, but the People that know God and feare him, shall be strong, he shall cover their heads in the day of Battaile, and they shall doe exploits, yet they that vnderstand among the People, and their Teachers that instruct them; these shall fall by the sword, and by flame and imprisonment; and by spoyle of their goods many dayes; yet feare none of these things, for hee that neither slumbers nor sleepes, will arise and take his owne quarrell into his hand, and you ſhall be holpen with a little helpe; Therfore truſt not in multitude of Forces, neither them that will cleaue to you with flatteries, for they will worke deceitfully, as they haue done in former times, nor expect a finall end of theſe perſecutions, Sathan will ſift, the tayle corne is his owne. If they call the Maſter of the houſe BELZEBUB, what reſpect can yee looke for that are of the houſhold. And the King ſhall do according to his will, and hee ſhall exalt himſelfe and magnifie himſelfe aboue every God, and ſhall ſpeake marvelous things againſt the God of Gods, great words againſt the moſt High, and ſhall weare out the Saints of the Moſt high, and thinke to change times and Lawes, and ſhall proſper till the indignation bee accompliſhed, for that, that is determined ſhall bee done, Neither ſhall he regard the God of his Fathers, nor deſire of Women, neither ſhall ſhe retaine the power of the Arme, being a branch of vngrafted Roots; nor regard any God, but ſhall magnifie himſelfe aboue all; In his eſtate hee ſhall honour the God of

Forces and Battell, being terrible to the servants of God and his Enemies; a God that his fore-fathers knew not; or an Altar shall he honour with Gold and Silver, and with Precious stones, and pleasant things; thus shall hee doe in the most strong holds with this God, a stranger for many yeares to the Apostles and their followers, whom he shall acknowledge and increase with glory; and hee shall cause in stead of Shepheards, Dogs and Wolues, in sheep-skins, to rule over many, as Lords over Gods heritage, and they shall not onely devide the Land for filthy lucre, but make Merchandizes of mens Consciences. But if GOD spared not the Angels, what shall become of these cursed Children, that haue not onely lost the Flocke, but gone astray and runne away themselues, following the way of BALAM the Son of BOZER, who loved the wages of vnrighteousnesse, having eyes full of Adultery; even when they speake their great swelling words of Vanitie and Absolution; at that time they allure to the Lusts of the Flesh, and much Wantonnesse, leading simple women into

Capti-

Captivitie,promising libertie,that are themselues the servants of Corruption, wallowing in the Myre like filthy Swine to cleanse themselues by wresting the Scriptures to their owne destruction, licking vp againe the vnsavorie meate themselues could ill disgest not long agoe, and running downe headlong into the deepe Lake of Fyre and Brimstone, whose latter end is worse then their beginning; it had beene better for these men to haue continued Heathens as they were at first in the pollutions of the world, then after they haue knowne the way of righteousnesse, to turne from it, crucifying the Sonne of God afresh, and putting him to open shame.

And at the time of the End shall the King of the South push at him, with all his Spanish Pikes, and the King of the North shall come against him like a whirlewinde, with Chariots and with Horsemen, and with many Ships, The Lord of Hosts send them Victorie; and he shall enter into the Countries, and shall overflow and passe over; hee shall enter also into the glorious Land *Domina gentium*, and many Countries ſhall be overthrowne; but theſe ſhall eſcape out of his hand, even *Edom* and *Moab*, and the chiefe of the Children of AMMON his Confederates, he ſhall ſtretch forth his hand alſo vpon the Countries, and the Land of *Egipt* ſhall not eſcape; But hee ſhall haue powers over the Treaſures of Gold and of Silver, and over all the Precious things of *Egipt*, and the *Libians* and the *Ethiopians* ſhall bee at his ſteps. But tidings out of the Eaſt and out of the North ſhall trouble him, therfore he ſhall goe forth with a great furie to deſtroy and vtterly to make away many; And hee ſhall plant the Tabernacles of his Cedars Pallace betweene the Seas in the glorious holy Mountaine; yet he ſhall come to his end, and none ſhall helpe him.

Therefore take vp a lamentation for the King of *Tyrus*, whoſe Cedars are for the building of both Houſes; and ſay thou haſt beene in EDEN the Garden of GOD; every pretious Stone to garniſh the foundation was thy Covering, the Ruby, the Topaz, and the Diamond, the Berill, the Onix, the

Iasper and the Saphire, these things were prepared for thee. Thou art annointed the Cherube that Covereth, thou wast vpon the holy Mountaine of GOD, and thou hast walked vp and downe in the middest of the Stones of Fyre: but because thou hast lifted vp thy heart, and said; I am GOD, I haue subdued three Kings. I sit in the middest of the Seas, and hast defiled thy sacred Houses, I will bring thee to Ashes, and none shall help thee. As I liue, saith the Lord, I will even doe according to thine anger, and according to thine Envie, which thou hast vsed out of thy hatred against them, and I will make my selfe knowne amongst them, when I haue judged thee, and thou shalt know that I am the Lord, and that I haue heard all thy Blasphemy, which thou hast spoken against the Mountaine of *Israell*, Saying, they are layd desolate by Massacre, they are given vs to consume by the sword; thus with thy mouth thou hast Boasted against Mee; therefore shortly when the whole Land of *Israell* reioyceth, I will make thee desolate, then thou shalt know that I the LORD doe Sanctifie

Israell, when my Sanctuary shall bee in the middest of them for ever.

Therefore, ô King of the North, arise from thy Throne, lay thy Royall Robe aside, and cause a Decree through *Tyrus* to be published; saying, Let them turne every one from his evill way, and from the violence or vnnaturall shedding of Blood, that is in their hands, &c. Who can tell if God will turne and repent, and turne away from his fierce anger, that wee goe not into Perdition.

DANIEL. Chap. XII.

Iames, Charles, — are Michaelss.

AND at that time shall Michael stand vp, the great Prince that defends the Faith, Charles King of Great *Britaine*, *France*, and *Ireland*, which standeth for the faithfull Children of our Nation, the Saints of the most Highest. As the Angell of God, so is my Lord the King, to discerne good and bad; therefore the Lord thy God will be with thee for ever.

And there ſhall be a time of trouble,ſuch as never was ſince there was a Nation, even to that ſame time, bleſſings and great felicities, being for the moſt part accompanied with Corrections, and extraordinary Calamities; Devotion and Religion of happineſſe, in this life the Higheſt, not exempt from ſuperſtition and hereſie; And at that time thy People ſhall bee delivered; Every one whoſe name is found written in the Booke,&c.

AL TRVTHS CESAR.

Behold the Lord is at the Dore, as a man come from a farre journey; All that ſleepe in the Duſt of the Earth, ſhall heare his voyce and awake,and come forth,thoſe that haue done good to the Reſurrection of life; Theſe haue their part in the firſt Reſurrection, and thoſe that haue done evill vnto the Reſurrection of Damnation. Then the Angell came downe from Heaven, hauing taken from the falſe Prophet the Key of the

Bottomlesse pit, having in his hand a great Chaine, hee shall next lay hold on the Dragon the Devill; and hee shall bee bound a Thousand yeares, or one day, which is all one with the Lord; he shall shut him vp, and set a Seale vpon him, for the wrath of the Lord that day, shall bee a sufficient marke that the Nations be deceived no more.

This Thousand yeares is the great day of the Lord, to poure out his wrath and just indignation vpon his Enemies; But the wise Virgins with Palmes in their hands, that haue not beene deceived by the subtilty or force of flatterers, shall shine in their Robes, as the brightnesse of the Firmament; Kings Daughters attended by honourable Matrons, as Starres for ever and ever, prepared for the Bridegroomes Marriage, whose Wife the Bride and Queene, hath made her selfe ready clothed in fine Linnen cleane and white, arrayed in a Garment of Needleworke wrought with Gold of Ophier, the Daughter of *Tyre* shall bee there with a Gift; she shall be brought to the King, with gladnesse and rejoycing, they shall enter into his

Pallace, ſaying, O King, thy Throne is for ever and ever, thou loveſt righteouſneſſe and hateſt wickedneſſe; therefore God thy God annoynt thee with gladneſſe aboue thy fellowes.

After this Thouſand yeares the great Day of the ſolemnitie finiſhed, the Bride being ſafe in her cloſſet and Marriage chamber, Sathan the olde Serpent ſhall be looſed a little ſeaſon, as Priſoners are ſet at libertie when they goe to the place of Execution to receiue his finall ſentence of everlaſting Damnation; yet hoping in his vaine imagination and hart that cannot repent to deceiue the Nations that are at reſt, to take a prey, to goe vp to the Citie that is in ſafetie that needs no Wall, neither the light of the Sunne or the Moone, &c.

Vnto whom the juſt Iudge frō his Throne of Glory with a terrible looke, for furie, jealouſie ſhall come vp into his face, ſhall ſay vnto him; Art thou he whom I haue ſpoken of in olde time by my ſervants the Prophets to giue the Nations warning of thee, how thou diddeſt not onely like a foole deceiue thy selfe, when thou saidst, I will ascend vp and be like the most highest, but like a cursed creature didst deceiue their innocent Parents, be prepared therefore, and prepare thy selfe and all thy Company, and see whether thou canst be a guard vnto them; or what defence they can make for themselues who could not be ignorant, and ought not to be carelesse, because by mine owne Mouth I gaue them warning, that after many dayes thou shouldst be visited and brought a Prisoner into the Land which is now brought backe from the Sword and cleansed, though it lay waste a time, and the Villages thereof vnwalled. For these I commanded them straightly to watch both concerning the things I fore-told them should come to passe; as also of this houre, lest like a Theefe, or as the Flood came vpon their fore-fathers the Vngodly, they should be surprised vnawares, because I told you of these things before depart, I know yee not, nor that Captaine your false Prophet, are yee those that eate my flesh and drinke my blood, whence are yee, I never knew you more, then you knew mine, or Me; cursed and deformed crew, with stiffe neckes, double crooked hearts, deafe Adders, and blinde People with eyes, goe yee cursed into everlasting fire.

Wee haue eaten and Drunke in thy presence, all the world was taxed by the Prince of our Nation; and thou hast taught in our streets; Their iniquitie is the greater, thrust them out. Lord, Lord, come out Dogs and Swine, Apes and Satiers, hence here all Lyers, Scoffers at the truth, vncleane persons, for here shall enter in no wise any thing that defileth, neither whatsoever worketh Abomination, or maketh a Lye, but they which are written in the Lambes Booke of Life.

But thou ô DANIEL, shut vp the words, and seale vp this Booke to the time of the end; Now that the whole world might take notice, and discerne when this Sealed Prophesie shall be opened, the time is more then once repeated, even at the time of the end, when the King of the South shall push at the King of the North, and the King of the North shall come against him like a Whirlewinde, for till then, though many shall run too and fro by the Art of Navigation, discovering an other Hemisphere, Sayling by the Compasse and the Needle, found out by expert men, and knowledge increased, furnishing Magnificent Libraries with printed Bookes, By which two Arts, chiefly the Gospell shall bee published to all Nations; yet the Character of this Booke shall not bee read, till the time of the end; which time is easie to be knowne, even without the Notice of the yeares closed vp in this Booke; where Eagles are gathered together, you suppose some Carcasse to be there: The Figtree, when her Branch is yet tender, and putteth forth her leaues, ye know that Summer is neere; *Ierusalem* when it was compassed with Armies, the Desolation was nigh. In like manner, when yee see these things come to passe fore-told you, know the end is nie, even at the dore; But of the day and houre knoweth no man, no not the Angells that are in Heaven; neither the Sonne but the Father; the accompt in this Booke of note, being by Centuries of yeares.

Then I Daniel looked, and behold

there ſtood other Two; the two Oliue Trees, the Tree of Life, either of them bearing Twelue manner of Fruites, the Two Witneſſes into whom, after Three dayes and a halfe, the Spirit of Life from God entred; and they ſtood vpon their feet. The one on this ſide of the banke of the River, and the other on that ſide of the bank of the River; The foũdations of the wall of the City, Ieſus Chriſt himſelf being the chiefe corner ſtone.

And one ſaid to the man clothed in Linnen, that was vpon the waters of the Rivers, that cryed with a loude voyce, as when a Lyon Roareth; Lord wilt thou at this time reſtore againe the Kingdome of *Iſraell*, how long ſhall it be to the end of theſe wonders, or tell vs when theſe things ſhall bee, and what ſhall bee the ſigne of thy comming, and of the end of the world.

And he held vp his right hand and his left hand to Heaven, ſhewing his Reſurrection and Aſcention, and ſware by him that Liveth for ever and ever, Heaven and Earth ſhall paſſe away, but my Word ſhall not paſſe, neither this froward generation, this

Nation till all these things bee done spoken of by my Mouth and the Prophets; there be some standing here, which shall not taste of Death, till they see the Sonne of Man comming in his Kingdome, his servants will fight for him. So shall even all my words be fulfilled.

It is not for you to know the times and seasons which the Father hath put in his owne power; But goe thou thy way and rest, and stand in the Lot. Seale vp those things which the Seven thunders vttered, and write them not, it shall be for a time and times and halfe, then all these things shall be finished, as a Henne gathereth her Chickens, or as a scattered Army in that day the Holy People shall be gathered together, in the meane time many shall bee purified and made white by the fiery Tryall; The wicked shall doe wickedly, and shall not vnderstand, but the wise, it is given vnto them to vnderstand the misteries of the Kingdome of Heaven.

And from the time that the daily Sacrifice shall bee taken away, or the yearely

Passeover by the destruction of *Ierusalem*, to place the Abomination that maketh desolate; there shall be a Thousand Two hundred and Ninetie dayes; Heere is the Measure of the Temple, and the Altar, and them that worship therein; And here is also the breach of the first Commandements, spoken of by our Lord; the abomination that maketh desolate not only the Sanctuary but the Citie; the first ripe Apples that hang so high against the Sunne; The Divell thought if hee could reach these, the rest were his owne; therefore to plucke them downe in the primitiue times, he began to reare his Ladder in the holy Places to set vp his plurality, adding the Images of living Mortall men to be worshipped with Divine honour, and vaine supplications, as if themselues were present, making no doubt, hauing no egresse and regresse in time to bring his owne amongst them into the nomber, in which expectation hee fayled not much; for who is this here, that sits in the Temple of God, as if there were Two Gods, besides his PIGMALION-like Image; the parts of which are ſeldome colde, if there bee heate in the Kiſſes of ſuch holy People.

The ſwiftneſſe of time is ſuch, I cannot gather all the Spices and dropping Myrrhe of this Tree, I can fixe no longer ſpeaking what manner God will ſit alone in his holy Temple, abhorring not only the people but the place where a Coleague is joyned with him in office; therefore of the next branch.

Suppoſe a man after his Marriage to a young Virgin, ſhould ſay, my experience is more then yours, I cannot alwayes walke hand in hand with you, neither may I keepe you in a Cloiſter that will not be for your health or my profit, neither muſt you forget your Covenant to bee ſubiect to my deſires not tending to the harme of either of vs; I loue you as mine owne Body, if I ſhould not loue you, I ſhould not loue my ſelfe, you are tender, and faire without blemiſh or blot, ſo I would haue your minde alſo without ſpot or wrinckle like your face, many ſtrangers will ſtriue to bee your Servants; not all for your beautie but ſome for malice and enuie to me: Though your intent be good in all things, yet because I am very jealous of mine honor, entertaine none in that manner; though they be silent for a time, and conceale themselues, in the end they will draw your affection from me; Besides, much resort though shee be never so chaste, is dalliance the marke of a knowne Harlot, which sort of women I would haue you differ from, and no marke I know more fit to put a difference betweene you then this; For much entertainment will not only waste our substance, better imployed vpon more necessary occasions, but consume time in vnprofitable idlenesse.

Is there no consequent, yes doubtlesse, I am the Lord thy God, thou shalt haue no other Gods but me; thou shalt not make Images of any likenesse to bowe or humble thy selfe before them; for of my honor I am a jealous God, you are mine, I bought you to enioy the libertie of my service, I brought yee out of the house of bondage, which no other God could doe; thou shalt loue the Lord thy God, and keepe his charge and his Statutes.

When yee goe forth to ſhew the way of truth to other Nations, this ſpirituall dalliance, which in the end turnes to whoredome, beware of it for it ſhall bee a marke betweene them that hate mee and you that keepe my Comandements; and though I will not at any time bee farre from you, yet you ſhall fall by Captivitie and perſecution to ſpread my name, or for the Triall of your Faith, when you ſee their Idolatrie pull downe their high Places, Preach againſt them; ſay, Little Children, ignorant people that vnderſtand not the ſlights of Sathan; Beware of Idols, tender natures encounter ſtrongeſt motions; Top-ſayles are firſt aſſaulted;. No man ſo well knowes his owne frailtie, as the Lord your God knowes how prone Devotion is to Superſtition.

Alſo when yee goe in and out amongſt the Heathen folke, or if the Lord giue them into your hands, as the *Amalikites* were given into the hand of the Children of *Iſraell*, when the Prophet ſaid; what meaneth this bleating in mine eares; SAULS excuſe ſhall not availe you; to ſay; we ſet them vp for Saints before the Lord, the Images of IUPITER for Iesus Christ; the Statue of HERCULES for CHRISTOPHER; VENUS and the little Lad, for the blessed Virgin, as holy as Scarcrowes in a Garden of Cowcumbers.

You that cannot make one haire white or blacke, will yee goe a Whoring after your owne inventions, to humble your selues before Pageants, Pictures, Images with eyes that see not, Eares without hearing, &c. More senslesse then a Beast; yet these rare Mamets, the light of the Sunne is too darke for them without Candles; when the Members of Christ goe naked, these must bee cloathed, not for warmnesse but for wantonnesse; and these are the Babyes made and dressed by the Divell, and decked to please his Children, abhorred, and abominable in the sight of the Lord.

Lastly, with these lines the Temple of God is Measured, and them that worship therein. Measuring is for Numbering; place is put for time, and sometimes space a thousand sixe hundred furlongs; Signifying the persecution of the Church so many yeares, reward her even as ſhe rewarded you. To riſe therefore and Meaſure the time, begin from the taking away of the daily Sacrifice or the Deſtruction of *Ieruſalem*, and count a thouſand two hundred and threeſcore yeares, wherein for the abſence of the Church in the Wilderneſſe, the two Witneſſes did Propheſie clothed in Sackcloth, ſo many yeares of Miſts and darkneſſe, to theſe muſt be added ſome dayes of faire weather, a hundred forty and foure thouſand, amounting to foure hundred yeares and odde, having their fathers name written in their foreheads, theſe ſing as it were a new ſong; Theſe are Virgins not (defiled with women) Chaſte converſation, not commanding laciviouſneſſe, by forbidding Marriage, waxing worſe and worſe.

The Temple was not built in a day, it is three Stories; the foure hundred yeares are to be devided into three ſeverall parts, Seventy yeares and odde, vntill the deſtruction of *Ieruſalem*, when the Apoſtles finiſhed their teſtimony, thirty yeares are reſtored for the raigne of CONSTANTINE the great, the remaines remaine for these last times, being the same eighteene thousand Measures spoken by EZEKIEL the Prophet, the Measure of the Temple within are not summed vp, I presume not to looke into the account, the Measure of it round about without, I heard the number of them cast vp, Eighteen thousand Measures, every Measure sixe Cubits, according to the Measure of a man. That is, of the Angell, three hundred yeares & odde; and the name of the City from that day shal bee God is there, that said Son of Man, the place of my Throne, and the place of the soles of my feet, where I will dwell in the middest of the Children of *Israell* for ever, and my holy Name shall the house of *Israell* no more defile, &c.

Blessed is he that waiteth and commeth to the thousand three hundred and fiue and thirty yeares, these are the blessed times of IOHN WICKLIFFE & IOHN Hus, both famous Martyrs, and burning Lights, set vp to shew forth the state and beauty of the truth, one burnt aliue, the other after hee was dead, being hard to judge in which of these, the Devill the Father of lyes, Antichrist his crucifying Sonne, and the Dragon, expressed most malice; from which cursed triplicitie, three Monsters of the bottomlesse Pit, God deliver vs, who will giue vs a Crowne of life; Come Lord IESUS, the grace of our Lord IESUS CHRIST bee with you all. Amen.

Last of all, the whole world is numbred and those that worke abomination therein, and the delights thereof, weighed in the balances, are found lighter then vanitie it selfe. There is nineteene yeares and a halfe to the day of Iudgement, Iuly the 28. M.DC.XXV. Sixe hundred and threescore Moneths are excluded, from this last Age of seventeene hundred yeares. And I thinke that I haue also the Spirit of God.

DANIEL.

Hee that is vniust and filthy let him bee so still, and hee that is righteous and holy, let him bee so still; for behold hee will come quickly, and his reward is with him. Blessed are they that doe his Commandements.

FINIS.

All the kings of the earth shall prayse thee (*STC* 903.5) is reproduced here, by permission, from the unique copy at the Public Record Office, Shelfmark SP 16/255/60–75. The size of the text-block of the original is 17.5 × 20 cm.

All the Kings of the earth ſhall prayſe thee, O Lord, for they haue heard the words of thy mouth; yea they ſhall ſing &c. xxviij. dayes, 138. Pſalme.

As ſeventy odd yeeres after the firſt Starre ſeen in the eaſt, followed the deſtruction of Ieruſalem, ſeventy ancients appointed to prophecy, ſo likewiſe the following Starre appearing 1572. ſeventy two yeeres, goeth before the end of the world, other ſeventy alſo two and two before him, before the daye of judgement.

To the renowmed Princes ELIZABETH, Queen of Bohemia, Princes Elect. Grace, gladnesse & peace.

Anagr. {PALIZGRAVE. ZAREP: VILAG.

YOVR Maiesties Throne, by degrees at lenght approaching humbly craue Royall patience, present the Man, greatly beloued, Daniel, intended to the King of chiefe memory your father, composed in a weeke (hastely) obtained not ccess, for with his fathers, the holy King was fallen a sleepe, his oule beyond mortall sight, taken vp to heaven, to partake imnortall crownation; a good fight having fought MICHAEL IAME CH. gainst the Babylonian Dragon, so many Euangelicall combats, nd controversies with the Beast. Lest their Goddesse Diana, her emple should be despised, no small stirre had with the craftsnen of Ephesus.

But what dost thou heere Eliiah, calleth your humble handnaide away. The children of your people have forsaken the Covenant, set vp altars, persecuted the Prophets, Iezebel taketh ossession of the vinyarde, friends of Naboth, and his bloode ryeth, Iehu and a Prophet to be anoynted, goe I must and re-

A turne,

turne, my errand onely to your Highnesse was to bring good tidings.

In the first yeere of Charles King of Great-Brittaine twenty eight of the moneth July, about six moneths after I began to vnderstand the visions of the Prophet Daniel, which hee saw in the first yeere of Belshacer, King of Babylon, a thing was revealed vnto mee, and the word was true, but the time appointed long (one and twenty hundred yeeres, three full weeks as it were) is now to be accomplished shortly, I eate no pleasant bread, was mourning full three moneths to vnderstand the visions.

One thousand six hundred twenty fiue, July twenty eight, early in the morning, about dawning of the daye, I heard these words from heauen, as it were a musicall voyce, coming downe, saying, There is nineteen yeeres & a halfe to the daye of iudgement, hee that testifieth these things, sayth surely I come quickely. Some few words more were vttered, as a Propheticall admonition vnto humility and meeknesse, dissolving within three dayes, former ambiguity. After which voyce the destroying Angell suddenly sheathed the sword, never so furiously drawne on that nation, for which blessing, and the happinesse to behold your face, and Royall progeny, walking in the trueth, honor, power and glory, be vnto him that sitteth vpon the Throne, even so come Lord IESUS. Amen, Amen.

AMSTERDAM 1633.
September 13.

ELEANOR • AVDELEY

REVEALE O DANIEL,

VII. Chap.

IN the first yeere of Belshacer, King of Babylon, Daniel had dreames and visions, and hee wrote the dreame and declared the summe of the matters.

I saw in my visions by night, and behold the fower windes of heauen strone vpon the great sea, and fower great Beasts came vp from the sea, divers one from another &c.

Interpretation followeth.

Windes are the spirit, purgeth all things, the swelling sea are the rebellious nations, of the fower parts of the earth, loosed windes, threating a wracke, dissolution of the world.

Fowet Beasts times and seasons displaying.

The first as a Lyon, beginneth from the birth of Iesus Christ, Revel.
persecuted by the Dragon, Lyon of the Tribe of Iuda, vnto the watchfull shepheards in the field proclaimed by Angells, wise men by a starre, by no inferior Prophet cryed in the wildernesse, to pull of his shoow, yet vnworthy, in triumph received with Hosanna, in the city, to witnesse whose Baptisme the holy Ghost descended, was by the Romane Monarchie (ouer all the world spreading her eagles winges) put to death, roote and seed of David, is recorded amongst these kings, King of kings, &c. whose enemies shall feele his hand, and his right hand, &c. Psalm 21.

The second beast like a Beare, and stood vpon the one side, signifying their election by voyces, and power of the Senat, had three ribbs in the mouth betweene the teeth, the moto this: And they said vnto him, arise and devoure much flesh, are three hundred yeeres, armes of the heathen Romane devouring times, whose raging raigne lasted so longe. In the infancy of which Empire, the massacred innocents, & Messiah suffered, Ierusalem was destroyed, that in Rome might be found the blood of Prophets & Saints, and of all that were slaine vpon the earth, dronken with the blood of Martyrs of IESUS.

The third Beast like a Leopard, that had vpon the backe of it fower winges, are fower hundred yeeres, beginning with the Beast, whose deadly wound was healed, raigne of Constantine the Great, so soone after spotted with Arrian leporisme, bearing fower heads, shewing the division of the Empire into so many parts when hee stood vp, held then too large and great for the government of one man.

The last Beast, the fourth, dreadfull, terrible, and strong exceedingly, had yron teeth, devoured & bracke in pieces, and stamped the residue with the feet thereof. Divers from all the Beasts before it, is Ecclesiastice Tyranny, pride of Prelats drawn from head to foote, had tenn hornes, shewing Antiquity of Antichrist, so many hundred yeeres, till the Ancient of dayes did sit.

The hornes farther considered (mother of harlots her coate) amongst which came vp another little horne, before whom three of the first were pluckt vp by the rootes; in this horne were eyes like the eyes of a man (watchfull in his owne behalfe) and a mouth (of an vngratfull ghuest) speaking presumtious things. The tenn Kings horns rising out of the head of the Beast, to know the trueth of them. The first Charles the Great, stiled *Christianissimi Romanorum Imperatoris*, the whole race of Childric pulled vp by the rootes made Rome for him, about a thousand

ſand yeeres ſince, abſolute Monarche of the Empire and all the dependances northward, for fower generations. The reſidue Spaniſh horns, ſince Charles the fift in defence of Romes (devourſed ſpowſe) no little champions.

The little horne, more ſtoute then his fellowes, whoſe mouth or language bewrayeth them, are the united French and Sweden forces, ſlaying the Antichriſtian Beaſt, and giuing his body to the burning flame, concerning the other Beaſts, though they inioyed their liues; had their dominion taken away, the reſidue ſtamped by Rome, vnder his feete, this little horne excepted.

Laſtly ſheweth the reſtoration of the kingdome of Chriſt, before the end of the world, and hee gaue him dominion and honor, and a Kingdome, that all people, nations, languages, ſhould ſerve him, his dominion is an euerlaſting Dominion, and ſhall never be taken away; and his Kingdome ſhall Antichriſt no more deſtroy.

The curſ't Beaſt hath a ſhorte horne, I beheld and the ſame horne made warre with the Saints, and prevailed againſt them; but the ancient of dayes came &c. the hayre of whoſe head like pure wolle, ſheweth his dayes infinite to be accounted, and the Kingdome, and the Dominion, and the greatneſſe of the Kingdome &c. And all powers ſhall ſerve & obey him. This is the end of the matter; and the contents of that which followeth.

CHAP. VII.

IN the first yeere of Belshazzar King of Babel,
Daniel saw a dreame, and there *were* visions in
his head, vpon his bedde: then he wrote the
dreame, and the declared the summe of the matter.
2 Daniel spake and said, I saw in my vision by
night, & behold, the foure windes of the heauen
stroue vpon *A* the great sea:
3 And foure great beastes came vp from the
B sea one diuers from another.
4 The first *was* as a *C* lion, aud had eagels
wings: I beheld till the wings thereof were pluckt
off, and it was lifted vp from the earth, and set
vpon *his* feet as a man, and a mans heart was giuen
him.
5 And behold, another beast *which was* the
second, was like a *D* beare, & stood vpon the one
side: and he had three ribs in his mouth betweene
his teeth, and they said thus vnto him, Arise, *and*
deuoure much flesh.
6 After this, I beheld, and loe, there *was* another like a *E* leopard, which had vpon his backe
foure wings of a foule: the beast had also foure
heads, and dominion was giuen him.
7 After this, I saw in the visions by night, and
behold, the *F* fourth beast *was* fearefull and terrible and very strong. It had great yron teeth: it
deuoured & brake in pieces, and stamped the residue vnder his feet: and it was vnlike to the
beasts that were before it: for it had ten hornes.
8 As I considered the hornes, beholde, there

A In the dayes of Noah to frame a new the micro-cosme, a hundred and twenty yeeres the spirit of God did strive no longer rested as it were.

B The nativity or rising of these fower beasts, or Kings vpon recorde one and twenty hundred yeeres compleat, added vnto the age of the World before, maketh a weeke of six thousand yeeres current.

C Sheweth when persecutiō for the Word began, the Vsher voyce leading the waye, Iohn beheaded for the word of God, first witnesse of Iesus, worshipped not the beast nor his image Herod, whose dauncing womā her picture is taken arrayed so in purple and pearle, in her hād a cup of gold &c.

D Called ten persecutions, continuing three hundred yeeres, first combat fought against the Mar-

B came

tyrs of Iesus by the reed Dragon with seuē heads, whose crownes mount vnto Romes foundation or Kings.

E The mungrell beast spoted with Arrian heresie so lately healed, signifying fower hundred yeeres his being on the wing.

F Fourth beast (Antichrist) hauing serued his apprentiship of seuen hundred yeeres, is free of the great city, setteth vp for himself ten horns his signe, yet not so grosely deceiuing the World, till a thousand yeeres were fullfilled.

came vp among them another little horne, before whom there were three of the first hornes
pluckt away: and behold, in his horne *were* eyes
like the eyes of man, and a mouth speaking presumptuous things.
9 I beheld till the thrones were set vp, and
the Ancient of dayes did sit, whose garment was
white as snow, and the haire of his head like the
pure wooll: his throne *was like* the fiery flame,
and his wheeles, *as* burning fire.
10 A fierie streame issued, and came foorth
from before him: thousand thousands ministred
vnto him, and ten thousand thousands stood before him: the iudgement was set, and the bookes
opened.
11 Then I beheld, because of the voyce of
the presumptuous words which the horne spake:
I beheld, euen till the beast was slaine, and his body destroyed, and giuen to the burning fire.
12 As concerning the other beasts, they had
taken away their dominion: yet their liues were
prolonged for a certaine time and season.
13 As I beheld in visions by night, behold,
one like the sonne of man came in the cloudes
of heauen, and approched vnto the Ancient of
dayes, and they brought him before him.
14 And he gaue him dominion, and honour,
and a kingdome, that all people, nations and languages should serue him: his dominion *is* an
euerlasting dominion, which shall neuer be taken away: and his dominion shall neuer be destroyed.
15 I Daniel was troubled in my spirit, in the

middes

middes of my body, and the visions of mine head
made me afraid.)

16 Therefore I came vnto one of them that
stood by, and asked him the trueth of all this: so
he told me, and shewed me the interpretation of
these things.

17 These great beasts which are foure, *are*
foure kings, which shall arise out of the earth,

18 And they shall take the kingdome of the
Saints of the most High, which shall possesse the
kingdome for euer, euen for euer and euer.

19 After this, I would *know* the trueth of the
fourth beast G which was so vnlike to all the
others, very fearefull, whose teeth were of yron,
and his nailes of brasse: *which* deuoured, brake
in pieces, and stamped the residue vnder his feet.

20 Also *to know* of the ten hornes that were
in his head, and of the other which came vp, before whom three fell, and of the horne that had
eyes, and of the mouth that spake presumptuous
things, whose looke was more stout then his fellowes.

G That Balam louing the wages of vnrighteousnesse Bishops (of Rome) their predecessor spurring the Beast, on whose progresse to attend, Satan is loosed, called for a little season, about seuen hundred yeeres a goe.

21 I beheld, and the same horne made battell
against the Saints, yea, and preuailed against them.

22 Vntill the Ancient of dayes came, and
iudgement was giuen to the Saints of the most
High: and the time approched, that the Saints
possessed the kingdome.

23 Then he said, The fourth beast shall be the
foorth kingdome in the earth, which shallbe vnlike to all the kingdomes, and shall deuoure the
whole earth, and shall tread it downe and breake
it in pieces.

24 And the ten hornes out of this kingdome
are ten Kings that ſhall riſe : and another ſhall
riſe after them, and he ſhallbe vnlike to the firſt,
and he ſhall ſubdue three Kings.

25 And ſhall ſpeake words againſt the moſt
High, and ſhall conſume *H* the Saints of the moſt
High, and thinke that he may change times and
lawes, and they ſhallbe giuen into his hand vntill
time, and times, and the diuiding of time.

26 But the *I* iudgement ſhall ſit, and they
ſhall take away his dominion to conſume and deſtroy it vnto the end.

27 And the *K* kingdome, and dominion, and
the greatneſſe of the kingdome vnder the whole
heauen ſhallbe giuen to the holy people of the
moſt High, whoſe kingdome *is* an euerlaſting
kingdome, and all powers ſhall ſerue and obey
him.

28 Euen this is the ende of the matter, I Daniel had many cogitations *which* troubled mee,
and my countenance changed in mee : but I kept
the matter in mine heart.

H Compaſſeth the tents of the ſaints, and fower quarters of the World, from Rochell to America.

I Ten hundred yeers writen in his horned fore head, expired, the Beaſt & the falſe prophet ſhallbe caſt into the lake &c.

K In his kingdome before the end of the world in earth raigning euē as in heauen.

DANIEL I END AL.

CHAP. VIII.

The reigne of Belſhacer about the age of the World 3425.

IN the third yeere of the reigne of king Belſhaz-
zar, a viſion appeared vnto mee, *euen* vnto mee
Daniel, after that *which* appeared vnto mee at
the firſt.

2 And I ſaw in a viſion, and when I ſaw it, I
was in the palace of Shuſhan, which is the prouince of Elam, and in a viſion me thought I was
by the riuer of Vlai.

3 Then

3 Then I looked vp and saw, and behold,
there stood before the riuer a A ramme which had
two hornes, and these two hornes *were* high: but
one was higher then another, and the highest
came vp last.
4 I saw the ramme pushing against the West,
and against the North, and against the South: so
that no beasts might stand before him, nor could
deliuer out of his hand, but he did what he listed
and became great.
5 And as I considered, behold, a goat came
from the West ouer the whole earth, and touched
not the ground: and this goate *had* an horne that
appeared betweene his eyes.
6 And he came vnto the ramme that had the
two hornes, whom I had seene standing by the
riuer, and ran vnto him in his fierce rage.
7 And I saw him come vnto the ramme, and
being moued against him, he smote the ramme,
and brake his two hornes: and there was no power
in the ramme to stand against him, but he cast
him downe to the ground, and stamped vpon
him, and there was none that could deliuer the
ramme out of his power.
8 Therefore the goate waxed exceeding
great, and when he was at the strongest, his great
horne was broken: and for it came vp foure that
B appeared toward the foure winds of the heauen.
9 And out of one of them came forth a little horne, which waxed C very great toward the
South, and toward the East, and toward the pleasant *land*.
10 Yea, it grew vp vnto the hoste of heauen,

A Ramme, leader of the flocke, goeing vp from washing. The Ramme signifieth the Romane Empire, the Empire of the Turks and Goths signified by the Gote, the two hornes Constantine & Rome.

B The fower kingdoms towards the fower winds of heaven, are the Westren Ilands of Great-Brittain, France, Spayne and the Turckesh Empire.

C The little horne coming forth of one of them, waxing great, is the forces of the French, shall thinke to change times & lawes, &c.

and it cast downe *some* of the hoste, and of the
starres to the ground, and trode vpon them.

11 And extolled himselfe against the prince
of the hoste, from whom the dayly *sacrifice* was
taken away, and the place of his Sanctuarie was
cast downe.

12 And a time shall be giuen *him* ouer the
dayly *sacrifice* for the iniquitie: and it shall cast
downe the trueth to the ground, and thus shall
it doe, and prosper.

13 Then I heard one of the Saints speaking;
D and one of the Saints spake vnto a certaine one,
saying, How long *shall endure* the vision of the
dayly *sacrifice*, and the iniquitie of the desolation to tread both the Sanctuary and the armie
vnder foote?

14 And he answered me, Vnto the euening
and the morning E two thousand and three hundreth: then shall the Sanctuary be cleansed.

15 Now when I Daniel had seene the vision,
and sought for the meaning, beholde, there stood
before me like the similitude of a man.

16 And I heard a mans voyce betweene *the
banks* of Vlai, which called, and saide, Gabriel,
make this man to vnderstand the vision.

17 So he came where I stood: and when hee
came, I was afraid, and fell vpon my face: but he
said vnto me, Vnderstand, O sonne of man: for
in the last time *shalbe* the vision.

18 Now as he was speaking vnto me, I being
asleepe *fell* on my face to the ground: but he touched me, and set me vp in my place.

19 And he said, Behold, I will shew thee what
shallbe

D Two saints, so called for gifts of the holy Ghost, precious in these dayes, the certain saint speaking, or wonderfull numberer of secrets, was a certaine childe about the age of 13 yeers in the yeere 1625 called Carr, of the nation of Great-Brittain, that for certaine mounths by signes E numbering foretold all things, beyonde relatiō, but being terrified and provoked to speake, lost the wonderfull gife for that time, after went beyonde sea.

E The dayes be so many yeeres to the end of the world, beginning frō the visiō was about the yeere of the world 3425.

ſhallbe in the laſt wrath: for the ende of the time
appointed *it ſhall come.*
20 The ramme which thou ſaweſt hauing
two hornes, *are* the Kings of the Medes and Per-
ſians.
21 And the goate *is* the King of Grecia, and
the great horne that is betweene his eyes, is the
firſt king.
22 And that that is broken, and foure ſtood
vp for it, *are* foure kingdomes, which ſhall ſtand
vp of that nation, but not in his ſtrength.
23 And in the end of their kingdome, when
the rebellious ſhalbe conſumed, a King of *F* fierce
countenance, and vnderſtanding darke ſentences,
ſhall ſtand vp.
24 And his power ſhallbe mightie, but not in
his ſtrength: and hee ſhall deſtroy wonderfully,
and ſhall proſper, and practiſe, and ſhall deſtroy
the mightie, and the people of the holy ones.
25 And through his policie alſo he ſhall cauſe
craft to proſper in his hand, and hee ſhall extoll
himſelfe in his heart, and by peace ſhall deſtroy
many: hee ſhall alſo ſtand vp againſt the prince
of princes *G*, but he ſhall be broken down without
hand.
26 And the viſion of the euening and the
morning, which is declared, is true: therefore
ſeale thou vp the viſion, for it *ſhallbe* after many
dayes.
27 And I Daniel was ſtricken and ſicke *certaine* dayes: but when I roſe vp, I did the kings
buſineſſe, and I was aſtoniſhed at the viſion, but
none vnderſtood it.

CHAP.

F Guſtavus Adolphus, king of Sweden, Goths & Wendals, making peace with Poland, came into Germany.

G Emperour, Prince of free Princes.

CHAP. IX.

IN the first yeere of Darius the sonne of Aha-
shuerosh, of the seede of the Medes, which was
made king ouer the realme of the Caldeans.
2 *Euen* in the first yeere of his reigne, I Daniel vnderstood by *A* bookes the number of the
yeeres, whereof the Lord had spoken vnto Ieremiah the Prophet, that he would accomplish *B* seuentie yeeres in the desolation of Ierusalem.
3 And I turned my face vnto the Lord God,
and sought by prayer and supplications with
fasting and sackcloth and ashes.
4 And I prayed vnto the Lord my God, and
made my confession, saying, O Lord God *which
art* great and fearefull, and keepest couenant
and mercie toward them which loue thee, and
towarde them that keepe thy commandements.
5 Wee haue sinned and haue committed iniquitie, and haue done wickedly, yea, we haue rebelled, and haue departed from thy precepts, and
from thy iudgements.
6 For wee would not obey thy seruauts the
Prophets, which spake in thy name to our kings,
to our princes, and to our fathers, and to all the
people of the land.
7 O Lord, righteousnes *belongeth* vnto thee,
and vnto vs open shame, as *appeareth* this day
vnto euery man of Iudah, and to the inhabitants
of Ierusalem, yea, vnto all Israel, *both* neere and
farre off, through all the countreys, whither thou
hast driuen them, because of their offences, that
they haue committed against thee.

A Bookes informing Daniel, concerning the yeeres of the captivity. So the Angell by the same numbers, or words, giueth him understanding.

B First that seventy weeks are determined &c. shewing seventy hundred yeeres, (or a weeke of thousands) from the begining to the end of the world, had not the dayes being shortned for the elects sake.

8 O Lord,

8 O Lord, vnto vs *apperteineth* open ſhame,
to our Kings, to our princes, and to our fathers,
becauſe wee haue ſinned againſt thee.

9 *Yet* compaſſion & forgiueneſſe *is* in the Lord
our God, albeit wee haue rebelled againſt him.

10 For we haue not obeyed the voyces of the
Lord our God, to walke in his lawes, which hee
hath laid before vs by the miniſtery of his ſer-
uants the Prophets.

11 Yea, all Iſrael haue tranſgreſſed thy Law,
and are turned backe, and haue not heard thy
voyce: therefore the curſe is powred vpon vs,
and the oathe that is written in the Law of Moſes
the ſervant of God, becauſe wee haue ſinned a-
gainſt him.

12 And he hath confirmed his words, which he
ſpake againſt vs, and againſt our iudges that iudged vs, by bringing vpon vs a great plague: for
vnder the whole heaven hath not beene the like,
as hath beene brought vpon Ieruſalem.

13 All this plague is come vpon vs, as it is written in the Law of Moſes: yet made wee not our
prayer before the Lord our God, that wee might
turne frõ our iniquities & vnderſtand thy trueth.

14 Therefore hath the Lord made readie the
plague, and brought it vpon vs: for the Lord our
God is righteous in all his works which he doth:
for we would not heare his voyce.

15 And now, O Lord our God, that haſt
brought thy people out of the lande of Egypt
with a mightie hand, and haſt gotten thee re-
nowne, as *appeareth* this day, we haue ſinned, wee
haue done wickedly.

16 O Lord, according to all thy righteousſ-
nes, I beseech thee, let thine anger and thy wrath
be turned away from the citie Ierusalem thine
holy Mountaine: because of our sinnes, and
for the iniquities of our fathers, Ierusalem and
thy people *are* a reproch to all *that are* about vs.
17 Now therefore, O our God, heare the prayer of thy seruant, and his supplications, and cause
thy face to shine vpon thy Sanctuarie, that lieth
waste for the Lords sake.
18 O my God, encline thine eare and heare:
open thine eyes, and behold our desolations, and
the citie wherevpon thy Name is called: for wee
do not present our supplications before thee for
our owne righteousnes, but for thy great tender
mercies.
19 O Lord heare, O Lord forgiue, O Lord
consider, and do it: deferre not, for thine owne
sake, O my God: for thy Name is called vpon
thy citie, and thy people.
20 And whiles I was speaking and praying,
and confessing my sinne, and the sinne of my people Israel, and did present my supplication before
the Lord my God, for the holy Mountaine of my
God.
21 Yea, while I was speaking in prayer, euen
the man Gabriel, whom I had seene before in
the vision, came flying, and touched me about the
time of the euening oblation.
22 And he informed *me*, and talked with me,
and said, O Daniel, I am now come forth to giue
thee knowledge *and* vnderstanding.

C Shewing seventy yeers after the going forth of the starre, seene by the wise men, Ierusalem should be destroyed vnto the ende (the weeke of weekes) for their bloody fact vnto Messiah their Prince, their pardon not sealed

23 At

23 At the beginning of thy ſupplications the
commandement came forth, and I am come to
ſhew *thee*, for thou art greatly beloued: therefore vnderſtand the matter and conſider the viſion.

24 *C* Seuentie weekes are determined vpon
thy people, and vpon thine holy citie, to finiſh
the wickedneſſe, and to ſeale vp the ſinnes, and
to reconcile the iniquitie, and to bring in euerlaſting righteouſnes, and to ſeale vp the viſion and
prophecie, and to anoint the moſt Holy.

25 Know therefore and vnderſtand that from
D the going foorth of the commaundement to
bring againe *the people*, and to builde Ieruſalem,
vnto Meſſiah the Prince, *ſhallbe* ſeuen weekes
and threeſcore and two weekes, *and E* the ſtreete
ſhallbe built againe, and the wall euen in a troublous time.

26 And after threeſcore and two weekes, ſhall
Meſſiah be ſlaine, and ſhall haue nothing, and
the people of the prince that ſhall come, ſhall deſtroy the citie and the Sanctuary, and the ende
thereof *ſhallbe* with a flood: and vnto the ende of
the battell it ſhallbe deſtroyed by deſolations.

27 *F* And he ſhall confirme the couenant with
many for one weeke: & in the mids of the weeke
hee ſhall cauſe the ſacrifice and the oblation to
ceaſe, and for the ouerſpreading of the abominations he ſhall make it deſolate, euen vntill the
conſumation determined ſhall be powred vpon
the deſolate.

till then, after in euerlaſting righteouſneſſe remaining, hauing their eyes opened to vnderſtand the viſions of the Prophets, concerning Chriſt Ieſus the moſt Holy.

D Informeth a ſecond ſtarre about ſeuẽty yeers before the ſecond coming of the Meſiah, the moſt high ſhould be ſent forth againe, appearing 1572.

E And that about threeſcore & two yeeres after Ieruſalem ſhould be reſtored againe, the ſtreet built in the ſtreits of a troubleſome time, deliuered from bloodguiltines, ſhould offer the ſacrifice of a troubled ſpirit, a contrite harte the true ſacrifice.

F In the middeſt of the great weeke the fourth thouſand yeere of the World (cauſed other oblation to ceaſe) the innocent Lambe of God was ſlaine.

CHAP. X.

IN the third yeere of Cyrus King of Persia, a
thing was revealed vnto Daniel (whose name
was called Beltešhazzar) and the word *was* true,
but the time appoynted *was* long, and he vnderstood the thing, and had vnderstanding of the vision.

2 At the same time I Daniel was in heauines
for three weeks of dayes.

3 I ate no pleasant bread, neither came flesh
nor wine in my mouth, neither did I anoynt my
selfe at all, till three weeks of dayes were fulfilled.

4 And in the foure and twentieth day of the
first moneth, as I was by the side of that great
riuer, euen Hiddekel.

5 And I lift mine eyes, and looked, and behold, there *was* a man cloated in linnen, whose
loynes were girded with fine gold of Uphaz.

6 His body also *was A* like the Chrysolite, and
his face (to looke vpon) like the lightning, and
his eyes as lampes of fire, and his armes and his
feete *were* like in colour to polished brasse, and
the voyce of his wordes *was* like the voyce of a
multitude.

7 And I Daniel alone saw the vision: for the
men that were with me, saw not the vision: but
a great feare fell vpon them, so that they fled
away and hid themselues.

8 Therefore I was left alone, and saw this
great vision, *B* and there remained no strength in
me: for my strength was turned in me into corruption, and I retained no power.

A Revealing after one and twenty hundred yeeres compleat from the vision, the mystery of the Word of God should be unsealed, when the seventh last trumpet should begin to sound, the mystery of God should be finished.

B The word of God revealed, is as gold and precious stones, as lightning going through the world as the voyce of a multitude, or army.

9 Yet

9 Yet heard I the voyce of his wordes : and
when I heard the voyce of his words , I slept on
my face, and my face *was* toward the ground.

10 And behold, an hand touched me, which
set me vp vpon my knees,and vpon the palmes of
mine hands,

11 And hee said vnto mee, O Daniel, a man
greatly beloued , vnderstand the words that I
speake vnto thee,and stand in thy place: for vnto
thee am I now sent. And when hee had said this
word vnto me, I stood trembling.

12 Then said he vnto mee, Feare not,Daniel:
for from the first day that thou diddest set thine
hart to vnderstand , and to humble thy selfe before thy God , thy words were heard , and I am
come for thy words.

13 But the prince *C* of the kingdome of Per-
sia withstood mee one and twenty dayes: but loe,
D Michael one of the chief princes,came to helpe
E me,and I remained here by the Kings of Persia.

14 Now I am come to shew thee what shall
come to thy people in the latter dayes : for yet
the vision *is* for *many* dayes.

15 And when he spake these words vnto me,
I set my face toward the ground , and held my
tongue.

16 And behold , one like the similitude of the
sons of man touched my lips : then I opened my
mouth , and spake , and sayd vnto him that stood
before mee , O my Lord , by the vision my sor-
rowes are returned vpon me , and I haue retained
no strength.

C Affliction allwayes companion of the word.
D Prince of Persia is the Dragon fighting against the Word of God, by Constātine the Great first defended.
E Sheweth after the vision one and twenty hundred yeeres full, Iames King of Great-Brittaine his wonderfull warre with the Dragon & his angells (false prophets (deceiuing the world) & Iesuits) so sharply contending for the body of Messiah, the tempter because hee could not turne stones into bread, would turne bread to Iesus body, the foode of the soule, whose word is indeed.

 For

17 For how can the seruaut of this my Lord
talke with my Lord *being* such one? for as for me,
straightway there remained no strength in mee,
neither is there breath left in me.

18 Then there came againe and touched me,
one like the appearance of a man, and he strengthened me.

19 And sayd, O man, greatly beloued, feare
not: peace *be* vuto thee: be strong and of good
courage. And when hee had spoken vnto mee, I
was strenthened, and sayd, Let my Lord speake:
for thou hast strengthened me.

20 Then sayd he, Knowest thou wherefore I
am come vnto thee, but now will I returne to
fight with the Prince *F* of Persia: and when I am
gone forth, loe, the prince of Grecia shall come.

21 But I will shew thee that which is decreed
in the Scripture of truth. *G* and there is none
that holdeth with mee in these things, but Michael your prince.

F Warre proclaimed against the Beast and the Dragō, besids the Turke his conquests, includeth allso the present destroying of the Romane state, by the Gothe, or he Gote. Gusta: Little Horne.

G Revelation scripture of truth xij. chap.

CHAP. XI.

ALso I, in the first yeere of Darius *A* of the
Medes, *euen* I stood to incourage & to strengthen him.

2 *B* And now will I shew thee trueth. Behold, there shall stand vp yet three kings in Persia, and the fourth shallbe farre richer then they
all: and by his strength, *and* by his riches he shall
stirre vp all against the realme of Grecia.

3 But a mighty King shall stand vp, that
shall rule with great domi nion, and doe according

A The first Christian Monarche Constantine, signified by Darius.

B His three sonnes or successors, by whose largess towards the Church of Rome, Bishops became so haughtie, stirred vp kings to warre against Turks, to leaue their Dominions vnder their Iuridiction.

ding to his pleaſure.
4 C And when he ſhall ſtand vp, his kingdome
ſhalbe broken, and ſhall be diuided toward the
foure windes of heauen: and not to his poſteritie,
nor according to his dominion, which he ruled:
for his kingdome ſhallbe pluckt vp euen *to be* for
others beſides thoſe.
5 D And the king of the South ſhallbe mighty,
and *one* of his princes, and ſhall preuaile againſt
him, and beare rule: his dominion *ſhallbe* a great
dominion.
6 E And in the end of yeeres they ſhalbe ioyned
together: for the Kings daughter of the South
ſhall come to the King of the North to make an
agreement, but he ſhall not retaine the power of
the arme, neither ſhal hee continue, nor his arme:
but ſhe ſhall be deliuered, and they that brought
her, and hee that begate her, and he that com-
forted her, in theſe times.
7 F But out of the bud of her rootes ſhall
one ſtand vp in his ſtead, which ſhall come with
an armie, and ſhall enter into the fortreſſe of the
King of the North, and doe with them *as he liſt*,
and ſhall preuaile,
8 And ſhall alſo cary captiues into Egypt their
gods with their molten images, *and* with their
precious veſſels of ſiluer and of gold, and he ſhall
continue moe yeeres then the king of the North.
9 So the king of the South ſhall come into
his kingdome, and ſhall returne into his owne
land.
10 Wherefore his ſonnes ſhallbe ſtirred vp,
and ſhall aſſemble a mightie great armie: and

one

C Charles the Great, for whom the naturall ſubiects of Childric by the Biſhops of Romes deſpenſation, were freed from their oath of obedience to his poſterity.

D House of Auſtrya their Imperiall Dominion.

E One thouſand ſix hundred expired, fruitleſs marriage between France & Spaine agreed, ſhe brought, deliuered them that brought her (ſent away without father, hauing an vnnaturall brother) not rare in theſe times.

F Rootes plurall, ſheweth inceſtious Auſtrian family.

one ſhall come, & ouerflow, and paſſe through:
then ſhall he returne, and be ſtirred vp at his fortreſſe.

11 And the King of the South ſhallbe angry,
and ſhall come foorth, and fight with him, with
the king of the North: for he ſhall ſet forth a
great multitude, and the multitude ſhallbe giuen into his hand.

12 *G* Then the multitude ſhallbe proude, and
their heart ſhall be lift vp: for hee ſhall caſt
downe thouſands: but he ſhall not *ſtill* preuaile.

13 *H* For the king of the North ſhall returne,
and ſhal ſet forth a greater multitude then afore,
and ſhall come forth (after certaine yeeres) with
a mightie armie, and great riches.

14 *I* And at the ſame time there ſhall many
ſtand vp againſt the king of the South: alſo the rebellious children of thy people ſhall exalt themſelues to eſtabliſh the viſion, but they ſhall fall.

15 So the King of the North ſhall come, and
caſt vp a mount, and take the ſtrong citie: and
the armes of the South ſhall not reſiſt, neither
his choſen people, neither *ſhall* there *be* any
ſtrength to withſtand.

16 But he that ſhall come, ſhall doe vnto him
as he liſt, and none ſhall ſtand againſt him: and
he ſhall ſtand in the pleaſant land, which by his
hand ſhalbe conſumed.

17 *K* Againe he ſhall ſet his face to enter with
the power of his whole kingdome, and his confederates with him: thus ſhal he do, & he ſhal giue
him the daughter of women to corrupt her: but
ſhe ſhall not ſtand *on his ſide*, neither be for him.

G French & Spaniſh warre, pride of the Empire.

H Lewes K. XIII. crowned, about which times Moores laſt were expelled.

I Spaine, many ſignifying the Dutche.

K Warre between France & England: daughter of woman, is giuen, daughter of Edward the IV daughter, whoſe Royall blood houſe of Lancaſter ſought to attaint or corrupt.

18 *L* After

18 *L* After this ſhall he turne his face vnto
the yles, & ſhal take many, but a prince ſhall cauſe
his ſhame to light vpon him, beſides that he ſhall
cauſe his owne ſhame to turne vpon himſelfe.

L Henry the VIII. king of England, for his owne behalfe rather, then Religiō, causeth the ſhamefull marriage of his brothers wife to turne on the B. of Rome.

19 For hee ſhall turne his face towardes the
fortes of his owne land: but hee ſhall be ouerthrowen and fall, and be no more found.

20 *M* Then ſhall ſtand vp in his place in the
glory of the kingdome, one that ſhall raiſe taxes:
but after few dayes he ſhall be deſtroyed, neither
in wrath, nor in battell.

M French kings, one deſtroyed by a ſplinter in his eye, neither in anger nor in battell, but a tillting ſporte, for a ſalte taxx his people rebelling.

21 And in his place ſhall ſtand vp vile perſon, to whom they ſhall not giue the honour of
the kingdome: but hee ſhall come in peaceably,
and obteine the kingdome by flatteries.

22 And the armes ſhalbe ouerthrowen with
flood before him, and ſhall be broken: and alſo
the prince of the couenant.

23 *N* And after the league *made* with him, hee
ſhall worke decietfully: for he ſhall come vp, and
ouercome with a ſmall people.

N Maſſacre, after the league.

24 He ſhall enter into the quiet and plentifull
prouince, and he ſhall doe that which his fathers
haue not done, nor his fathers fathers: he ſhall
diuide among them the pray and the ſpoyle, and
the ſubſtance, yea, and he ſhall forecaſt his de-
uiſes againſt the ſtrong holds, euen for a time.

25 Alſo he ſhall ſtirre vp his power, and his
courage againſt the King of the South, with a
great armie, and the King of the South ſhall be
ſtirred vp to battell with a very great and mighty
army: but he ſhall not ſtand: for they ſhall fore-
caſt and practiſe againſt him.

O Henr. IV. French king with a small people ouercame, for a time a Protestāt, was destroyed by them, who did eat a portion of his meat, escaping so many enemies, denying the verity of the Lords Supper, first stabbed in the mouth, after at the hart, whose hart was against the holy couenant, dyed richer then happy.

26 O Yea, they that feede of the portion of his
meate, shall destroy him: and his armie shall ouerflow: and many shall fall, and be slaine.
27 And both these Kings harts *shallbe* to doe
mischiefe, and they shall talke of deceit at one
table: but it shall not auaile: for yet the ende
shallbe at the time appointed.
28 Then shall hee returne into his land with
great substance: for his hart shallbe against the
holy couenant: so shall he doe and returne to his
owne land.
29 At the time appointed hee shall returne,
and come toward the South: but the last shall not
be as the first.
30 For the shippers of Chittim shall come a-
gainst him: therefore he shallbe sorie and returne,
and fret against the holy couenant: so shall hee
doe, he shall euen returne and haue intelligence
with them that forsake the holy couenant.
31 And armes shall stand on his part, and
they shall pollute the Sanctuary of strength, and
shall take away the dayly *sacrifice*, and they shall
set vp the abominable desolation.
32 And such as wickedly breake the couenant, shall he cause to sinne by flatterie: but the
people that doe know their God, shall preuaile
and prosper.
33 And they that vnderstand among the people, shall instruct many: yet they shall fall by
sword, and by flame, by captiuitie and by spoyle
many dayes.
34 Now when they shall fall, they shallbe
holpen with a little helpe: but many shall cleaue
vnto them fainedly.

And

35 And ſome of them of vnderſtanding ſhall fall
to try them, and to purge, & to make them white,
till the time be out: for there *is* a time appointed.
36 And the king ſhall doe what him liſt: he
ſhall exalt himſelfe, and magnifie himſelfe againſt
all, *that is* God, and ſhal ſpeake marueilous things
againſt the God of gods, and ſhall proſper, till
the wrath be accompliſhed: for the determina-
tion is made.
37 P. Neither ſhall he regard the God of his
fathers, nor the deſires of women, nor care for any
God: for he ſhall magnifie himſelfe aboue all.
38 But in his place ſhall he honour the god
Mauzzim, and the god whom his fathers knew
not, ſhall he honour with gold and with ſiluer, and
with precious ſtones, and pleaſant things.
39 This ſhall he doe in the holdes of Mauzzim with a ſtrange God whom he ſhall acknowledge: hee ſhall increaſe *his* glory, and ſhall
cauſe them to rule ouer many, and ſhall diuide
the land for gaine.
40 And at the ende of time ſhall the king of
the South puſh at him, and the king of the North
ſhall come againſt him like whirlewinde with
charets, and with horſemen, and with many
ſhips, and hee ſhall enter into the countreyes,
and ſhall ouerflow and paſſe through.
41 He ſhall enter alſo into the pleaſant land,
and many *countreyes* ſhalbe ouerflowen: but theſe
ſhall eſcape out of his hand, *euen* Edom and Moab, and the chiefe of the children of Ammon.
42 He ſhall ſtretch forth his hands alſo vpon
the countreys, and the land of Egypt ſhall not
eſcape.

P Remaineth the warre, conſuming the Saints of the moſt High by famine, & proſperous exploicts againſt Spaine & others, by Lewes the laſt French King.

43 But he ſhall haue power ouer the treaſures
of golde and of ſiluer, and ouer all the precious
things of Egypt, and of the Libyańs, and of the
blacke Mores where he ſhall paſſe.

44 But the tidings out of the Eaſt & the North
ſhall trouble him: therefore hee ſhall goe forth
with great wrath to deſtroy and roote out many.

45 And he ſhall plant the tabernacles of his
palace betweene the ſeas in the glorious *and* holy
mountaine, yet he ſhal come to his end, and none
ſhall helpe him.

CHAP. XII.

Anagr. { IAMES CHARLES.
ARE MICHAELSS. }

A The Angell preſenteth the new mā Michael great Prince, King of Great-Brittaine.

B The plague and other grieuances.

C To be bleſſed or accurſied, all awake in the graue, Michael Archangell ſounding the trumpet.

D Convertors of the Heathen vnto them is giuen a crowne of ſtarres, addition to their glory.

E The viſion ſealed vp till the end, allſo the admirable arte of Navigation and Printing to be then invented.

AND at that time ſhall Michael *A* ſtand vp, the
great prince, which ſtandeth for the children
of thy people, & there ſhalbe a time of *B* trouble,
ſuch as neuer was ſince there began to be a nation
vnto that ſame time: and at that time thy people
ſhallbe deliuered, euery one that ſhall be found
written in the booke.

2 And many of them that *C* ſleepe in the duſt
of the earth, ſhall awake, ſome to euerlaſting life,
and ſome to ſhame and perpetuall contempt.

3 And they that be wiſe, ſhall ſhine, as the
brightnes of the firmament: and they that turne
many to righteouſneſſe, *ſhall ſhine* as the ſtarres,
D for euer and euer.

4 But

4 But thou, O Daniel, *E* ſhut vp the words, &
ſeale the booke till the end of the time: many ſhal
run to and fro, and knowledge ſhall be increaſed.
5 Then I Daniel looked, and behold, there
ſtood other two, the *F* one on this ſide of the
brinke of the riuer, and the other on that ſide of
the brinke of the riuer.
6 And *one* ſayd vnto the man clothed in linen, which was vpon the water of the riuer, When
ſhalbe the end of theſe wonders?
7 And I heard the man clothed in linen which
was vpon the waters of the riuer, when hee held
vp his *G* right hand and his left hand vnto heauen,
and ſware by him that liueth for euer, that *it ſhall
tary* for a time, two times and parte: and when he
ſhall haue accompliſhed to ſcatter the power
of the holy people, all theſe things ſhallbe finiſhed.
8 Then I heard it, but I vnderſtood it not:
then ſaid I, O my Lord, what ſhallbe the end of
theſe things?
9 And he ſayd, *H* Go thy way Daniel: for the
words are cloſed vp, and ſealed, till the end of the
time.
10 Many *I* ſhallbe purified, made white, and
tried: but the wicked ſhal doe wickedly, & none
of the wicked ſhall haue vnderſtanding: but the
wiſe ſhall vnderſtand.
11 And from the time that the dayly *ſacrifice*
ſhallbe taken away, and the abominable deſolation ſet vp, there *ſhallbe* a thouſand, two hundred
and ninety dayes.

F From the birth or Baptiſme of IESVS Chriſt, ſupported (on either ſide the riuer Iordaine) with Prophets and Apoſtles, in them reuealed how lõg to the end of the world.

C Confirmed with his oath, whoſe foote and hand meaſured out all, that the time alotted vnto them, is ſeuenten hundred yeeres, a time, and times, & halfe (or part) ſo long time of Chriſtianity is meaſured, which accompliſhed, the ſcattered Iewes ſhallbe brought home.

H Daniell againe aſſured, at the end theſe words ſhould be reuealed.

I Martyrdom for the Word of God ſhewed, and after long darkeneſſe, the light thereof ſhould ſhine againe, after Ieruſalems deſtruction, a thouſand two hundred and ninety yeers.

12 Blessed *is he* that K waiteth and commeth
to the thousand, three hundreth and fiue & thirty dayes.
13 But goe thou thy way till the end *be*: for
thou shalt rest and stand vp in thy lot, at the end
of the dayes.

K Dayes of Iohn Wicliff, and forty fiue yeeres after that, much more: Dayes of Iohn Huß, and Ierrom of Prague blessed Martyrs, purified & tryed &c. But goe thou thy way, till the End Daniel I end all, rest.

1633.

Blessed that waiteth and commeth vnto 1645.

Printed at AMSTERDAM,
CIↃ IↃ C XXXIII.

Woe to the House (*STC* 904.5) is reproduced here, by permission, from the copy at the Public Record Office, Shelfmark 16/255/59. The size of the textblock of the original is 31.25 × 21.25 cm.

Woe to the Houſe.

Interpretation.

Anagr. { ELIZABETH STANLEY.
THAT IEZEBEL SLAIN.

Anagr. { ANA STANLEY.
A LYE SATANN.

SO ſhe wrote letters in Ahabs name, and ſealed them with his ſeale, and ſent the letters vnto the El-ders, and to the Nobles that were in the city. She wrote in the letters &c. Set two men ſonns of Beliall before him, to beare witneſſe againſt, ſaying, &c. And the men of the city, the Elders, and the Nobles who were the inhabitants of the city, did as Iezebel had ſent vnto them. And there came two men, children of Belial, and the men of Belial witneſſed.

Decembris 1626. Aprilis 1631.

Before St. Henry Martin, Judge of the prerog:

Appeared perſonely S[r]. George Haſtings of Middleſex K. Knight, and Thom:aſs Gardner of the middle Temple Eſqu-lyer, and by vertu of their Corp. oath made, ſaith &c.

And behold the word of the Lord came to Eliiah, ſaying, Ariſe meet Ahab &c. Haſt thou killed, and allſo taken poſſeſſion, in the place, &c. and the doggs ſhall eat Iezebel by the walls of Izeerel.

And when hee came, behold the Captaines of the hoaſt were ſitting, and hee ſaid, I haue an errand to thee, O Captaine. And Iehu ſaid, To which of vs all? And hee ſaid, to thee, O Captaine. And when Iehu was come to Izeerel, Iezebel heard of it, and ſhe painted her face, and tyr'ed her head, and looked out of a window, &c. And hee troade her vnder foote.

Anagr. { MERVIN AVDELEY.
MEVEL VINEYARD.

NO, No, my vineyard FOWNTH-IL doe account,
A fruitfull h-il, from Tower hil did mount,
My ſoule from Lyons, thence on Angels wings
In Abrahams boſome Haleluiah ſing.

ISAIAH 5.

Now will I ſing, to my beloued, a ſonge of my beloued to his vineyard, my beloued &c.

Printed at AMSTERDAM, Anno M.DC.XXXIII.